THE COMPLETE
VEGETARIAN
COOKBOOK

350 Simple and Meat-Free Recipes for a Healthy Lifestyle
and Diet - Make Delicious Vegetarian Meals
with 5 Ingredients or Less

TABLE OF CONTENTS

INTRODUCTION

What does it mean to be a vegetarian?

A Vegetarian is a person who does not eat meat, poultry, or fish. Vegetarians eat only plant foods such as fruits, vegetables, legumes, and grains or products made from them. Some people think of a vegetarian as a person who does not eat red meat but may consume fish and chicken. Other people consider a vegetarian to be someone who avoids eating all animal flesh, including fish, poultry, and red meat. However, "true" vegetarians avoid the consumption of all meats, including fish and chicken.

Vegetarianism is not a new concept; it has been practiced since ancient times in India during the Vedic period (1500-500 BC) as well as in Greece and Rome. It continues to be practiced today in modern society around the world. In most cases, it is a matter of individual choice.

Eating meat and fish has been a common practice all over the world for thousands of years. In some cultures, the preparation of the meat or fish symbolizes wealth and luxury, while in others it represents a source of survival. Today, people are becoming more aware of the impact that their food choices have on their health as well as on the environment.

Why do people become vegetarians? The reasons vary widely from person to person. Some people object to the cruelty and suffering of animals raised for food. Some people object to the environmental effects of producing meat and fish. Others become vegetarians because they believe animal flesh is unhealthy to eat or because they believe it is unspiritual or unwise. For some, it is a choice of economic necessity.

How often should you eat fruits and vegetables? The recommendation is to eat five servings per day based on a 2,000 calorie diet. One serving is equal to one-half cup raw or one cup ready-to-eat. Fruits and vegetables provide vitamins, minerals, fiber, and other nutrients that are essential for good health. It is recommended that most Americans make fruits and vegetables the basis of their diet; ideally, they should be eaten at every meal.

So, specifically, what are the foods that one needs to avoid? These are as follows:

- Beef

- Pork

- Lamb

- Veal

- All Game (deer, elk, etc.)

- Any other land mammal that's been fed animal products or by-products such as eggs and dairy (many land mammals are herbivores)

- Fish and Shellfish

- Goose and Duck

- Emu and Alligator

- Any other animal that is not a seafood product

- Animal by-products such as gelatin (e.g., gummy bears)

As a vegetarian, what specific foods do you avoid? For starters, you can limit your consumption of the following:

- Pork and bacon

- Eggs (or eat only eggs that are certified organic or non-cage free)

- Dairy products (or consume only dairy products that are certified organic)

- All products that are made from animals, such as leather shoes, belts, jackets, etc.

What are the substitutes that you use to replace the meat and fish that you avoid?

- Tofu (made from soybeans)

- Tempeh (made from soybeans)

- TVP (textured vegetable protein)

- Seitan (very high in protein, available as steak strips or chicken-style pieces)

- Soy Nuggets/Sausage

Being a vegetarian has its benefits, but there are definitely some challenges as well. If you are considering the option of being a vegetarian, the most important thing to consider is your overall health. However, if you have concerns with the lack of protein in your diet, believe that it's unwise to eat only plant products, or simply crave meat and fish and think you can't give them up without feeling hungry or deprived, then the choice of becoming a vegetarian may not be the right one for you.

This vegetarian cookbook will help you get a delicious and healthy recipe on the table that will make your life less stressful. A good recipe doesn't need a long list of ingredients to make it tasty, and while preparing meals may seem hard. You can eat together a healthy family food in the same amount of time you'd need to order takeout!

This vegetarian cookbook will show you a variety of dishes you can make with easy-to-find ingredients. This is the perfect practical guide for anyone looking to make a variety of delicious meals that are healthy. It includes recipes for breakfast, lunch, dinner, appetizers, and desserts, as well as those for snacks and sides. Whether looking to lose weight or just eat more healthily, this cookbook will make it easier than ever before!

So, let us begin the journey.

CHAPTER 1:

BREAKFAST RECIPES

1. Mexican Breakfast Burritos

Preparation Time: 10 minutes

Cooking Time: 5 minutes

Servings: 6

Ingredients:

- 1 batch Perfect Scrambled Eggs
- 1 cup canned black beans, rinsed
- 1 cup shredded Cheddar cheese
- 6 (10- to 12-inch) flour tortillas
- ¾ cup Three-Minute Blender Salsa or your favorite jarred salsa, plus more for serving
- Optional: Sour cream and guacamole for serving

Directions:

1. Follow the recipe for Perfect Scrambled Eggs. Stir in the beans and cheese in the last 2 minutes of cooking.

2. Warm the tortillas in the microwave for about 10 seconds, so they are pliable. Add some of the egg filling to the center of each tortilla. Top with a few spoonfuls of salsa. Wrap the burritos tightly. Serve and enjoy!

Nutrition: Calories: 147 Carbs: 8g Fat: 4g Protein: 10g

2. Scrambled Eggs

Preparation Time: 5 minutes

Cooking Time: 5 minutes

Servings: 4

Ingredients:

- 8 large eggs
- ½ teaspoon salt, plus more for seasoning
- 2 tablespoons water
- 2 tablespoons salted butter
- Black pepper

Directions:

1. Crack eggs into a bowl and whisk rapidly with salt and water for 30 seconds, or until the eggs are blended together and start to foam.

2. Melt the butter on low heat in a medium nonstick skillet. When the butter bubbles, add egg mixture to the pan.

3. The eggs will start to cook in about 30 seconds. As they begin to get firm around the edges of the pan, use a heatproof rubber spatula to push them to the center of the pan. Stir as the eggs form large curds—soft but solid pieces of boiled egg within the liquid egg mixture. Remove the pan from the stove when all the eggs are firm but still soft and no visible liquid remains. Cooking should be about 2 to 3 minutes.

4. Season with salt and pepper to taste.

5. Technique Tutorial: Whisking the eggs incorporates air into them, so the more muscle you use in whisking, the lighter and fluffier the eggs will be.

Nutrition: Calories: 295 Carbs: 9g Fat: 21g Protein: 19g

3. Spinach Feta Quiche

Preparation Time: 10 minutes

Cooking Time: 50 minutes

Servings: 6

Ingredients:

- 10-ounce package frozen spinach
- 1 cup whole milk
- 5 large eggs
- 6 ounces crumbled feta cheese with Mediterranean herbs (or plain)
- 1 refrigerated pie crust, brought to room temperature

Directions:

1. Preheat the oven to 350°F.
2. Drain all the water and squeeze out of the spinach. You can use a colander for this.
3. In a bowl, mix the spinach, milk, eggs, and cheese.
4. Unroll pie crust and then press it into a 9- to 10-inch pie plate. Crimp the edges with a fork (press the ends of the fork tines down on the rim, making sure to go around the whole rim) and make sure the pie crust is uniform all around the rim.
5. Pour egg in the pie crust, making sure not to overfill.
6. Bake it for 45-50 minutes until the quiche is set. Make sure the crust is golden brown around the edges. Poke it using a toothpick. To know that this is already done, it should come out clean.
7. Cool for 10 to 20 minutes before serving.
8. Simple Swap: If you prefer, use 10 ounces of fresh baby spinach in place of frozen spinach. Chop it and sauté. Pour olive oil into a skillet and put it on medium-high heat until wilted. The idea is to cook it until most of the water is removed. It can then be added to the egg mixture in step 3.

Nutrition: Calories: 141 Carbs: 9g Fat: 9g Protein: 7g

4. Raspberry Lemon Yogurt Parfaits

Preparation Time: 5 minutes

Cooking Time: 0 minutes

Servings: 4

Ingredients:

- 2 cups raspberries, plus 4 extra raspberries, for garnish
- 4 (6-ounce) containers lemon yogurt
- ½ cup granola
- 2 tablespoons sliced or chopped almonds

Directions:

1. Divide the raspberries evenly into four parfait glasses. Top each with half a container of yogurt.
2. Sprinkle each with granola. Top with the remaining yogurt. Sprinkle the almonds on top.
3. Garnish with the extra raspberries and serve.
4. Prep Tip: If you do not have parfait glasses, you can use cocktail or

highball glasses. Small mason jars work too. It won't really matter what you put the parfaits in because as soon as you serve them, they will disappear.

Nutrition: Calories: 168 Carbs: 30g Fat: 3g Protein: 5g

5. Peanut Butter Banana Smoothie

Preparation Time: 5 minutes

Cooking Time: 0 minutes

Servings: 4

Ingredients:

- 4 small frozen ripe bananas, peeled and sliced
- 2 cups 2% milk
- 8 ounces vanilla Greek yogurt
- ¼ cup smooth peanut butter
- 1 cup ice

Directions:

1. Add the bananas, milk, yogurt, peanut butter, and ice to a blender. Blend it for 2-3 minutes, or until the mixture is smooth.

2. If you don't have a blender, put all the ingredients in a large bowl and using an electric mixer until all lumps are gone at low speed. If the mixture is smooth, but large pieces of ice remain, just pick them out with a spoon before transferring the smoothies to glasses.

3. Serve in tall glasses with straws.

4. Prep Tip: To store bananas in the freezer, peel and slice the bananas and seal each banana individually in a small freezer bag. Take them out when ready to use.

Nutrition: Calories: 229 Carbs: 31g Fat: 10g Protein: 7g

6. The Runner's Drink

Preparation Time: 10 minutes

Cooking Time: 0 minutes

Servings: 1

Ingredients:

- 2 teaspoons chia seeds
- 1¼ cups water
- Juice of 1 lemon or lime
- Drizzle of pure maple syrup

Directions:

1. Shake or stir together the chia seeds, water, and citrus juice. Sweeten with a drizzle of maple syrup.

2. Pour over ice and serve.

3. Substitution Tip: Add ¼ cup of frozen berries for a more tropical drink. Let them sit for 30 minutes to defrost before adding to the drink.

Nutrition: Calories: 84 Fat: 4g Carbohydrate: 10g Protein: 2g

7. Blueberry and Grape Brainiac Smoothie

Preparation Time: 5 minutes

Cooking Time: 0 minutes

Servings: 4

Ingredients:

- 2 cups blueberries

- 2 cups seedless red or black grapes
- 4 cups unsweetened almond milk
- 2 tablespoons pure maple syrup
- 4 tablespoons ground flaxseed
- 1 cup ice cubes

Directions:

1. In a blender or food processor, purée everything together until smooth.

2. Ingredient Tip: Smoothie recipes are surprisingly simple to make and customize. Just remember this simple formula: fruit + nondairy milk + healthy fat like nuts, avocado, or seeds + ice. Optional add-ins include leafy greens for iron and folate, one frozen banana for extra potassium and vitamin C, a sweetener like a maple syrup, and a sugar-free protein powder.

Nutrition: Calories: 242 Fat: 11g Carbohydrate: 32g Protein: 6g

8. Overnight Chia Seed Plant-Powered Breakfast

Preparation Time: 5 minutes

Cooking Time: 0 minutes

Servings: 3

Ingredients:

- ½ cup chia seeds
- 2 cups unsweetened almond milk or any unflavored, unsweetened non-dairy milk
- 3 tablespoons pure maple syrup
- ½ teaspoon vanilla extract

- Toppings of your choice: fruits, nuts, seeds, figs, dates, toasted coconut flakes (optional)

Directions:

1. In a container with a lid, thoroughly combine the chia seeds, almond milk, maple syrup, and vanilla. Refrigerate overnight until it becomes thick and pudding-like.

2. When you're ready to serve, stir to remove any clumps. Spoon into bowls and customize your breakfast by adding your favorite toppings. I like to include a sweet and crunchy element. Drizzle with a little extra maple syrup, if you'd like.

Nutrition: Calories: 397 Fat: 21g Carbohydrate: 46g Protein: 10g

9. Baked Oatmeal and Fruit

Preparation Time: 5 minutes

Cooking Time: 20 minutes

Servings: 4

Ingredients:

- 3 cups quick-cooking oats
- 3 cups unflavored, unsweetened nondairy milk
- ¼ cup pure maple syrup
- 1 tablespoon vanilla extract
- 1 to 2 cups blueberries, raspberries, or both

Directions:

1. Preheat the oven to 375°F.

2. In a large mixing bowl, combine all the ingredients. Put everything in a

large bowl, then cover it with aluminum foil.

3. Bake for 10 minutes, then bake for another 5 to 10 minutes uncovered, or until all the liquid is visibly gone and the edges start to brown.

4. Let cool 5 minutes before serving. Serve with an extra splash of non-dairy milk and a drizzle of maple syrup.

5. Leftovers: Make a big batch as a quick go-to breakfast for the week. Just reheat in the oven or microwave or on the stovetop.

Nutrition: Calories: 365 Fat: 7g Carbohydrate: 67g Protein: 9g

10. <u>Hemp and Oat Granola</u>

Preparation Time: 5 minutes

Cooking Time: 30 minutes

Servings: 4

Ingredients:

- 2 cups old-fashioned rolled oats
- 1½ teaspoons cinnamon
- ½ cup hemp seeds
- ⅓ Cup slivered almonds
- ⅓ Cup pure maple syrup

Directions:

1. Preheat the oven to 350°F. Line large baking sheet using parchment paper.

2. Spread the oats on the lined baking sheet. Sprinkle over the cinnamon and toss. Spread evenly on the baking sheet and toast in the oven for 10 minutes.

3. Add the hemp seeds and toss them with the oats. Toast for another 10 minutes. Add the almonds, toss, and toast for another 5 minutes.

4. Take it off the oven and drizzle with maple syrup. Toss, spread evenly on the baking sheet, and toast for another 5 minutes.

5. Refrigerate covered for up to 5 days.

6. Substitution Tip: Substitute sunflower seeds for the hemp seeds or add ½ cup chopped dates or dried fruit.

Nutrition: Calories: 434 Fat: 20g Carbohydrate: 49g Protein: 17g

11. <u>Quick Green Posole</u>

Preparation Time: 10 minutes

Cooking Time: 3 minutes

Servings: 4

Ingredients:

- 6 ounces (about 5) tomatillos, hulled, washed, and quartered
- ½ jalapeño, seeded and ribs removed, roughly chopped
- 1 small yellow onion, roughly chopped
- 2 (15-ounce) cans hominy, drained
- 1 cup vegetable broth
- 1 teaspoon ground cumin
- ½ teaspoon chili powder
- 1 teaspoon garlic powder
- ½ teaspoon dried oregano
- ¼ teaspoon kosher salt, plus more for seasoning

Directions:

1. Put the tomatillos, jalapeño, and onion in a blender and pulse to chop all the ingredients into a chunky purée. Pour mixture into the pressure cooker pot. Add the hominy, vegetable broth, cumin, chili powder, garlic powder, oregano, and salt.

2. Lock the pressure cooker and then set the timer for 3 minutes at low pressure. When the timer is off, quick release the pressure. Stir the mixture to recombine, add additional salt if needed, and serve immediately.

Nutrition: Calories: 289 Carbs: 37g Fat: 10g Protein: 16g

12. Harvest Ratatouille

Preparation Time: 15 minutes

Cooking Time: 3 minutes

Servings: 4

Ingredients:

- 2 tablespoons extra-virgin olive oil, divided

- 2 large yellow onions, diced

- 1 teaspoon garlic powder

- 1 teaspoon dried thyme

- 1 teaspoon dried oregano

- ½ teaspoon kosher salt, plus more if needed

- 1 eggplant, cut into 1-inch chunks

- 2 red bell peppers, seeded and diced

- 2 summer squash, sliced

- 1 (28-ounce) can whole tomatoes, in juice

- ¼ teaspoon freshly ground black pepper

Directions:

1. With the pressure cooker on the brown or sauté setting, heat 1 tablespoon of olive oil until it shimmers. Add the onions and sauté, stirring frequently, until they are softened and translucent, about 5 minutes. Stir in the garlic powder, thyme, oregano, and salt. Add the eggplant, bell peppers, and squash, and pour the tomatoes and their juices over the vegetables without stirring.

2. Lock the lid, then set the timer for 3 minutes at high pressure. When the timer is off, quick release the pressure. Gently stir the ingredients, drizzling in the remaining 1 tablespoon of olive oil, and season it with salt and pepper if needed. Serve hot or warm.

Nutrition: Calories: 189 Carbs: 15g Fat: 12g Protein: 3g

13. Green Thai Tofu and Veggie Curry

Preparation Time: 15 minutes

Cooking Time: 3 minutes

Servings: 4

Ingredients:

- 1 (14-ounce) block extra-firm tofu

- 2 red bell peppers, seeded and sliced

- 1 red onion, sliced

- 8 ounces green beans, trimmed into 1-inch
- 1 (14-ounce) can prepare green curry

Directions:

1. Slice the tofu lengthwise, then cut each piece into 1-inch cubes. Add the tofu, peppers, onion, and green beans to the pressure cooker pot. Pour curry sauce over the tofu and vegetables and stir lightly to combine.

2. Lock lid and set the timer for 3 minutes at high pressure. When the timer is off, quickly release the pressure. Stir to combine and serve immediately.

Nutrition: Calories: 170 Carbs: 8g Fat: 14g Protein: 6g

14. <u>Indian Chickpea Curry</u>

Preparation Time: 10 minutes

Cooking Time: 3 minutes

Servings: 4

Ingredients:

- 1 tablespoon vegetable oil
- 1 medium yellow onion, sliced
- 2 tablespoons red curry paste
- 1 (13.5-ounce) can coconut milk
- 2 teaspoons cornstarch
- 2 cups canned chickpeas or 2 cups Basic Chickpeas
- 4 carrots, peeled and sliced

Directions:

1. With the pressure cooker on the brown or sauté setting, heat the vegetable oil until it shimmers. Sauté the onion and stir frequently, until it is softened and translucent, about 5 minutes. Stir in the curry paste and sauté, stirring constantly, for 1 minute. Stir in the coconut milk.

2. Place the cornstarch in a small bowl. Add a spoonful or two of warm liquid from the pot to the bowl and use a fork or spoon to make a loose paste. Stir cornstarch mixture back into the pot. Then add the chickpeas and carrots to the pot.

3. Lock lid and set the timer for 3 minutes at high pressure. When the timer is off, quickly release the pressure. Stir the curry and serve hot.

Nutrition: Calories: 332 Carbs: 55g Fat: 8g Protein: 10g

15. <u>Spaghetti Squash with Pesto and Fresh Mozzarella</u>

Preparation Time: 10 minutes

Cooking Time: 7 minutes

Servings: 4

Ingredients:

- 2 (3-pound) spaghetti squash
- 1 cup water
- ½ cup prepared pesto
- 8 ounces fresh mozzarella cheese, cubed
- 2 cups quartered cherry tomatoes

Directions:

1. Slice the stem end of the spaghetti squash and cut it into quarters. Use a spoon to get the seeds and the pulp.

2. Place a rack or a steamer insert in the pressure cooker pot and add the water to the pot. Place the squash on the rack or steamer, cut-side down. The squash can be layered on top of each other, but shouldn't fill the pot more than two-thirds full. If it doesn't all fit, cook it in two batches.

3. Lock lid and set the timer for 7 minutes at high pressure. When the timer is off, quick release the pressure, open the cooker, and remove the squash with tongs.

4. If squash is cool enough to handle, use a fork to scrape the squash into strands, transferring them to a large bowl. Spoon the pesto over the squash, and use tongs to toss the squash, distributing the pesto to evenly coat the squash. Add the mozzarella and cherry tomatoes, and toss to combine. Serve warm or at room temperature.

Nutrition: Calories: 190 Carbs: 12g Fat: 10g Protein: 12g

16. Speedy Scratch Mac 'n' Cheese

Preparation Time: 10 minutes

Cooking Time: 5 minutes

Servings: 4

Ingredients:

- 8 ounces elbow macaroni
- 1 cup evaporated milk, divided
- 1¼ cups water
- 1½ teaspoons kosher salt
- 1 teaspoon dried mustard
- 1 egg
- 8 ounces extra-sharp Cheddar cheese, grated
- 1½ teaspoons cornstarch

Directions:

1. In the pot pressure cooker, add the macaroni, ¾ cup of evaporated milk, water, salt, and dried mustard. Stir to combine.

2. Lock lid and set the timer for 5 minutes at high pressure.

3. Meanwhile, in a small bowl, whisk the egg. Add ¼ cup of evaporated milk and whisk to combine.

4. Place the grated cheese in a medium bowl and sprinkle the cornstarch over the cheese. Toss to coat.

5. When the pressure cooker timer goes off, quick release the pressure. Test the macaroni, if it is not quite done, switch the setting to sauté or brown, and simmer it for 1 to 2 minutes, covered, until tender.

6. If you haven't switched the setting, switch the setting to sauté or brown and add the milk-egg mixture and a large handful of cheese. Stir to melt the cheese. Continue adding the cheese in several handfuls, stirring until it completely melts with each addition. Serve immediately.

Nutrition: Calories: 367 Carbs: 40g Fat: 16g Protein: 13g

17. <u>Steamed Broccoli or Cauliflower, Four Ways</u>

Preparation Time: 10 minutes

Cooking Time: 2 minutes

Servings: 4

Ingredients:

- 1 broccoli head, cut into bite-size florets (about 4 cups) or 1 cauliflower head, cut into bite-size florets (about 4 cups)
- 1 tablespoon extra-virgin olive oil
- 2 tablespoons melted unsalted butter
- ¼ cup toasted bread crumbs
- 2 tablespoons balsamic vinaigrette
- 2 tablespoons grated parmesan cheese
- Salt and pepper

Directions:

1. Place a steamer insert in the pot of a pressure cooker. Add the water to the pot. Place the broccoli or cauliflower in the insert.
2. Lock lid and set the timer for 2 minutes at high pressure. When the timer is off, quick release the pressure and open the lid. Use tongs to transfer the broccoli or cauliflower to a serving dish.
3. Top or toss broccoli with one of the following:
4. 2 tablespoons melted unsalted butter and ¼ cup toasted bread crumbs that have been mixed with 2 tablespoons grated Parmesan cheese. Season with salt and pepper.
5. 1 tablespoon extra-virgin olive oil and ¼ cup crumbled feta or goat cheese. Season with salt and pepper.
6. 1 tablespoon extra-virgin olive oil. Then sprinkle it with red pepper flakes, salt, and pepper.
7. 2 tablespoons prepared or homemade balsamic vinaigrette

Nutrition: Calories: 68 Carbs: 9g Fat: 3g Protein: 1g

18. <u>Steamed Artichokes</u>

Preparation Time: 10 minutes

Cooking Time: 15 minutes

Servings: 4

Ingredients:

- 4 medium artichokes
- 1 lemon, halved
- 1 cup water

Directions:

1. To prepare the artichokes, use kitchen shears to trim the spiky tips off all the artichoke leaves. Pull any tough leaves off the very bottom and use a paring knife to trim off the stem. Rub cut parts of the artichoke with the lemon to avoid discoloring.
2. Place a steamer insert or a rack in the pressure cooker pot.
3. Add the water to the pot. Arrange the artichokes in the pressure cooker, stacking them if necessary.
4. Lock lid and set the timer for 15 minutes at high pressure.

5. When the timer is off, quick release the pressure, open the lid, and remove the artichokes with tongs. Serve hot or cool or use in another recipe.

Nutrition: Calories: 27 Carbs: 6g Fat: 0g Protein: 2g

19. <u>Steamed Asparagus, Four Ways</u>

Preparation Time: 5 minutes

Cooking Time: 1 minute

Servings: 4

Ingredients:

- ½ cup water
- 1 pound asparagus, trimmed
- 2 tablespoons melted unsalted butter mixed
- ½ teaspoon freshly grated lemon zest
- 2 tablespoons champagne vinaigrette
- 1 tablespoon slivered almonds
- ¼ cup hollandaise sauce
- 1 tablespoon hazelnut oil
- 1 tablespoon chopped hazelnuts
- Salt and pepper

Directions:

1. Place a steamer insert in the pot of a pressure cooker. Add the water to the pot. Place the asparagus in the insert. If the stalks are too long, it's fine to lean them against the sides of the cooker.
2. Lock the lid and then set the timer for 1 minute at high pressure. When the timer is off, quick release the pressure

and open the lid. Transfer the asparagus to a plate.

3. Top or toss asparagus with one of the following:
4. 2 tablespoons melted unsalted butter mixed with ½ teaspoon freshly grated lemon zest
5. 2 tablespoons champagne vinaigrette and 1 tablespoon slivered almonds
6. ¼ cup hollandaise sauce
7. 1 tablespoon hazelnut oil and 1 tablespoon chopped hazelnuts. Season with salt and pepper.

Nutrition: Calories: 32 Carbs: 3g Fat: 1g Protein: 5g

20. <u>Seasoned Bok Choy</u>

Preparation Time: 5 minutes

Cooking Time: 1 minute

Servings: 4

Ingredients:

- 1 cup water
- 4 baby bok choy heads, quartered lengthwise
- 1 tablespoon rice wine vinegar
- 1 teaspoon sesame oil
- 1 tablespoon toasted sesame seeds

Directions:

1. Place a steamer insert in the pot of a pressure cooker. Add the water to the cooker and mound the bok choy in the steamer.
2. Lock lid and set the timer for 1 minute at high pressure. When the timer is off, quick release the pressure and

remove the cover, transfer the bok choy to the platter or bowl.

3. In the bowl, whisk together the vinegar and sesame oil. Drizzle it over the bok choy. Sprinkle the sesame seeds over the bok choy and serve immediately.

Nutrition: Calories: 13 Carbs: 2g Fat: 0g Protein: 2g

21. Spicy Kale

Preparation Time: 1 minute

Cooking Time: 5 minutes

Servings: 4

Ingredients:

- 1 tablespoon extra-virgin olive oil
- 2 garlic cloves, minced
- 1 kale bunch, stemmed and chopped or 1 (1-pound) bag chopped kale
- 1½ cups water
- 1 tablespoon red wine vinegar
- ½ teaspoon red pepper flakes
- ¼ teaspoon kosher salt

Directions:

1. With the pressure cooker on the sauté or brown setting, heat the olive oil. Add the garlic and sauté for 30 seconds, stirring constantly. Add the kale and water to the pressure cooker.

2. Then lock the lid and set the timer for 5 minutes at high pressure. When the timer is off, quick release the pressure, remove the lid, and toss the cooked greens with the vinegar, red pepper flakes, and salt.

3. Serve hot.

Nutrition: Calories: 65 Carbs: 1g Fat: 1g Protein: 1g

22. Stewed Collard Greens

Preparation Time: 10 minutes

Cooking Time: 20 minutes

Servings: 4

Ingredients:

- 1 tablespoon vegetable oil
- 1 yellow onion, diced
- 1 collard greens bunch, roughly chopped
- 2 cups vegetable broth
- 1 teaspoon smoked paprika
- 1 tablespoon cider vinegar
- ½ teaspoon hot sauce
- ⅛ teaspoon kosher salt
- ⅛ teaspoon freshly ground black pepper

Directions:

1. With the pressure cooker on the sauté or brown setting, heat the vegetable oil until it shimmers. Stir the onion and stir it frequently until it is softened and translucent, about 5 minutes. Add the collard greens, vegetable broth, and paprika.

2. Lock lid and set the timer for 20 minutes at high pressure. When the timer is off, naturally release it for 10 minutes. Then totally remove the lid after.

3. Stir in the vinegar, hot sauce, salt, and pepper. Serve hot.

4. To prepare the collard greens, rinse the leaves well by immersing them in a sink full of cool water. Fold leaves in half along the stem and use a chef's knife to cut away the toughest part of the stem. Then stack a few leaves at a time, roll them up into a cigar shape, and slice them into wide ribbons. You can further chop the ribbons if desired.

Nutrition: Calories: 30 Carbs: 6g Fat: 0g Protein: 2g

23. Green Beans, Four Ways

Preparation Time: 10 minutes

Cooking Time: 2 minutes

Servings: 4

Ingredients:

- 1 cup water
- 4 pounds green beans, trimmed
- Salt and pepper
- 2 teaspoons extra-virgin olive oil
- 2 tablespoons finely grated parmesan cheese
- 1 cup mixed sliced mushrooms
- ¼ cup packaged fried onions
- ¼ cup toasted slivered almonds
- 2 teaspoons sesame oil over
- 1 tablespoon toasted sesame seeds

Directions:

1. Add the water to the pressure cooker pot. Place a steamer insert in the cooker. Place the beans in the steamer insert.

2. Lock lid and set the timer for 2 minutes at high pressure. When the timer is off, quick release the pressure and open the lid. Use tongs to transfer the beans to a serving bowl.

3. Season the beans with one of the following:

4. Toss beans with salt, pepper, 2 teaspoons extra-virgin olive oil, and 2 tablespoons finely grated Parmesan cheese.

5. Place 1 tablespoon of unsalted butter on the hot beans and add salt and pepper. Toss with tongs to melt the butter and coat the beans. Sprinkle with ¼ cup toasted slivered almonds.

6. Drizzle 2 teaspoons of sesame oil over the beans and add salt and pepper. Toss the beans with tongs to coat them with the oil. Sprinkle the toasted 1 tablespoon sesame seeds on the top of the beans.

7. Sauté 1 cup mixed sliced mushrooms in butter until softened, 6 to 7 minutes. Stir the mushrooms into the beans and add salt and pepper. Top with ¼ cup packaged fried onions.

8. To prepare green beans, break or trim the ends off each bean. You can do this by lining up a handful of beans on the cutting board and using a sharp knife to cut off all the ends at once.

Nutrition: Calories: 40 Carbs: 9g Fat: 0g Protein: 2g

24. Maple-Glazed Carrots

Preparation Time: 8 minutes

Cooking Time: 2 minutes

Servings: 4

Ingredients: 1 cup water

- 1 pound baby carrots
- 1½ tablespoons unsalted butter
- 1½ tablespoons pure maple syrup
- ¼ teaspoon kosher salt
- Pinch freshly ground black pepper
- 1 teaspoon fresh minced thyme

Directions:

1. Place the water and carrots in the pot of a pressure cooker.

2. Then lock the lid and set the timer for 2 minutes at high pressure. When the timer is done, release quickly the pressure, open the cooker and switch to the brown setting.

3. Put the butter, maple syrup, salt, and pepper, then sauté the carrots for 2 to 3 minutes or until the remaining liquid almost evaporates. Sprinkle with fresh thyme. Serve hot or warm.

Nutrition: Calories: 110 Carbs: 0g Fat: 4g Protein: 1g

25. Beets, Two Ways

Preparation Time: 10 minutes

Cooking Time: 12 to 16 minutes

Servings: 4

Ingredients:

- 1 cup of water
- 1 pound medium-size beets, root, and stems trimmed

For Version 1

- 2 tablespoons unsalted butter
- 2 tablespoons granulated sugar
- 2 tablespoons apple cider vinegar
- ⅛ teaspoon kosher salt
- Pinch freshly ground black pepper

For Version 2

- 2 tablespoons unsalted butter
- ⅛ teaspoon kosher salt
- Pinch freshly ground black pepper
- ¼ cup finely grated Parmesan cheese
- 1 tablespoon minced fresh parsley

Directions:

1. Place a steamer insert or a rack in the pot of a pressure cooker. Add the water to the cooker. Place the beets on the steamer insert.

2. Lock on the lid and then set the timer for 13 minutes at high pressure, less if the beets are very small. When the timer is done, release the pressure and open the lid. Check the beets using a fork; the fork should easily pierce the beets, which should still be firm but a bit of softness when squeezed. If they still seem very hard, like an uncooked potato, lock the lid back on and cook at high pressure for 3 more minutes.

3. When the beets are ready and cooked, remove them from the cooker with tongs and let them rest until cool enough. Slip off the skins from the beets, they should come right off.

Quarter the beets and slice into bite-size pieces.

4. To prepare version 1, remove the rack and pour the water out of the pressure cooker. With the setting on sauté or brown, melt the butter. Add the sugar and vinegar and then stir until the sugar dissolves. Add the beets and stir to coat them evenly with the vinegar mixture. Add the salt and pepper. Serve hot or warm. (Note: If you want to serve this recipe chilled, replace the butter with extra-virgin olive oil; otherwise, the butter will congeal.)

5. To prepare version 2, place the hot sliced beets into a bowl and toss with the butter, salt, and pepper. When the butter is already melted, and it coats the beets, add now the Parmesan and parsley and toss to distribute.

Nutrition: Calories: 154 Carbs: 20g Fat: 6g Protein: 5g

26. Crust less Spinach Quiche

Preparation Time: 10 minutes

Cooking Time: 5 hours

Servings: 6

Ingredients:

- Nonstick cooking spray
- 4 large eggs
- 1 cup half-and-half
- 1 cup shredded sharp Cheddar cheese
- 3 cups fresh baby spinach leaves
- 2 cups cubed ham
- ½ teaspoon salt
- ¼ teaspoon freshly ground black pepper

Directions:

1. Prepare a nonstick slow cooker and spray it with cooking spray.

2. In a large bowl, beat the eggs. Add the half-and-half, Cheddar cheese, spinach, ham, salt, and pepper, and stir to combine. Pour the mixture into your slow cooker.

3. Cover your slow cooker. Cook for 5 hours on low or 3 hours on high.

4. Turn off the slow cooker and let it sit for 15 minutes before serving.

5. Empty a box of frozen spinach into a colander. Run warm water over the spinach until it's warm. Use a clean a paper towel or a towel to press down on the spinach and release as much water as possible.

Nutrition: Calories: 381 Total Fat: 27g Fat: 14g Cholesterol: 277mg Carbohydrates: 7g Fiber: 1g Protein: 27g

27. Blueberry-Coconut Quinoa

Preparation Time: 10 minutes

Cooking Time: 3 hours

Servings: 4

Ingredients:

- ¾ cup quinoa, rinsed and drained
- ¼ cup shredded unsweetened coconut
- 1 tablespoon honey
- 1 (13.5-ounce) can coconut milk
- 2 cups fresh blueberries

Directions:

1. Put the rinsed quinoa in the slow cooker. Sprinkle the coconut over the top and then drizzle with the honey.

2. Open the can of coconut milk. Stir until smooth and even in consistency. Pour over the quinoa.

3. Cover your slow cooker and cook for 3 hours on low.

4. Stir the quinoa, then scoop it into four serving bowls. Top each bowl with blueberries and serve.

5. If fresh blueberries are out of season or aren't available, you can easily substitute frozen blueberries, which are available year-round.

Nutrition: Calories: 468 Total Fat: 33g Carbohydrates: 43g Fiber: 7g Protein: 8g

28. Apple-Cinnamon Oatmeal

Preparation Time: 10 minutes

Cooking Time: 4 hours

Servings: 4

Ingredients:

- 1 cup steel-cut oats
- 1 tablespoon unsalted butter, melted
- 4 cups water
- ¼ cup brown sugar
- 1 teaspoon ground cinnamon
- ½ teaspoon salt
- 1 Granny Smith apple, peeled, cored, and chopped
- ½ cup milk

Directions:

1. Combine the steel-cut oats and butter in the slow cooker. Stir the oats until it is coated with the butter. Add the water, brown sugar, cinnamon, and salt.

2. Cover your slow cooker for it to cook for 4 hours at low.

3. Stir the chopped apple into the oatmeal. Scoop into four serving bowls and serve with a splash of milk.

Nutrition: Calories: 143 Total Fat: 4g Cholesterol: 10mg Sodium: 329mg Carbohydrates: 25g Fiber: 3g Protein: 3g

29. Mini Frittatas

Preparation Time: 5 minutes

Cooking Time: 5 minutes

Servings: 2

Ingredients:

- 3 eggs
- ½ cup coconut milk
- ½ teaspoon salt and pepper
- ¼ cup kale
- ¼ cup chopped broccoli
- 1 cup of water

Directions:

1. Mix eggs, milk, kale, broccoli, salt, and pepper and mix in a dish.

2. Pour mixture into individual baking molds using silicone molds.

3. Place molds on a rack in Instant Pot with 1 cup of water.

4. Set Instant Pot to Manual and High Pressure for 5 minutes.

5. When the timer goes off, and cooking is done, perform a quick steam release.

6. Enjoy!

Nutrition: Calories 242 Fat 20.9g Saturated Fat 14.7g Cholesterol 246mg Carbohydrate 5.8g Fiber 1.9g

30. Breakfast Hash

Preparation Time: 5 minutes

Cooking Time: 5 minutes

Servings: 2

Ingredients:

- 1 tablespoon coconut oil

- 2 small sweet potatoes, peeled if desired

- 2 eggs

- 1/4 cup water

- 1 cup shredded parmesan cheese

Directions:

1. Set the Instant Pot to "Sauté" and add a thin layer of coconut oil to the bottom of the pan. While the Instant Pot is heating, finely shred the sweet potatoes in a food processor. Squeeze out any excess moisture, then add the shredded sweet potatoes to the hot oil. Let the sweet potatoes brown in the hot oil without stirring.

2. Meanwhile, beat the eggs and set them aside.

3. Once the sweet potatoes have browned on the bottom, break them

up with a wooden spoon. Add the water, eggs, parmesan cheese, stir gently.

4. Lock the cover on the Instant Pot and bring it to High Pressure. Let cook for 1 minute and then use the Quick-release method to release the steam.

5. Serve the breakfast hash immediately.

Nutrition: Calories 344 Fat 14.4g Cholesterol 174mg Carbohydrate 42.7g Fiber 6.2g

31. Swiss Chard Muffin

Preparation Time: 5 minutes

Cooking Time: 10 minutes

Servings: 2

Ingredients:

- 2 eggs

- 1/8 teaspoon pepper seasoning

- 4 tablespoons shredded goat cheese

- 1 green onion, diced

- ½ cup Swiss chard chopped

- 1 1/2 cups water

Directions:

1. Put the steamer basket in the Instant Pot and add 1 1/2 cups water.

2. Break eggs into a large measuring bowl with pour spout, add pepper, and beat well. Divide the cheese, Swiss chard, and green onion evenly between silicone muffin cups. Pour the beaten eggs into each muffin cup and stir with a fork to combine.

3. Place muffin cups on a steamer basket. Cover and lock lid in place. Select High Pressure and 8 minutes

cook time. When the timer beeps, turn off, wait two minutes, then use a quick pressure release.

4. Carefully open the lid, lift out the steamer basket, and remove muffin cups.

5. Serve immediately.

Nutrition: Calories 66 Fat 4.7g Cholesterol 89mg Carbohydrate 0.8g Fiber 0.2g

32. Nutmeg Banana Quinoa

Preparation Time: 10 minutes

Cooking Time: 5 minutes

Servings: 2

Ingredients:

- 1 cup quinoa
- 1 cup soy milk
- 1 cup of water
- 2 bananas
- 1 teaspoon nutmeg
- 1 tablespoon honey

Directions:

1. Add in the quinoa, soy milk, and water in Instant Pot.

2. Slice up 1 of the bananas and add it into the Instant Pot. Add in nutmeg and honey. Stir.

3. Set the Manual button to 5 minutes. Once the timer beeps, let the pressure release naturally for 10 minutes and then carefully release the rest of the pressure. Be careful, though, since grains can really get foamy.

4. Stir the quinoa and scoop into bowls. Slice the second banana and add fresh slices to the top of each bowl.

Nutrition: Calories 522 Fat 8.1g Cholesterol 0mg Carbohydrate 98.4g Fiber 10g

33. Cabbage Soup

Preparation Time: 10 minutes

Cooking Time: 20 minutes

Servings: 2

Ingredients:

- 1 head cabbage
- ½ tablespoon dried basil
- 2 oz Cheddar cheese chunks
- ½ tablespoon coconut cream
- ½ teaspoon garlic powder
- Salt to taste

Directions:

1. Add all ingredients to the blender pitcher and lock the lid.

2. Select the "Soup" setting for 20 minutes.

3. Garnish with shredded cheddar cheese and serve.

Nutrition: Calories 213 Fat 10.5g Cholesterol 29mg Carbohydrate 21.8g Fiber 9.1g

34. Lime Ginger Green Beans

Preparation Time: 5 minutes

Cooking Time: 15 minutes

Servings: 2

Ingredients:

- 2 cups green beans, cut into 4 inches

- 1 cup water
- 1 tablespoon vegetable oil
- 2 teaspoons freshly squeezed lime juice
- ½ teaspoon salt
- 1 teaspoon ginger powder

Directions:

1. Place the green beans in a steamer basket and put the basket into the Instant Pot. Add the water. Lock the lid and turn the steam release handle to sealing. Using the Manual or Pressure Cook function, set the cooker to Low Pressure for 15 minutes.

2. When the cooking time is complete, quickly release the pressure.

3. In a serving bowl, stir together the vegetable oil, lime juice, salt, and ginger powder.

4. Carefully remove the lid and add the green beans to the bowl. Toss to combine. Taste and add the remaining lemon juice or ginger as needed.

Nutrition: Calories 121 Fat 7g Cholesterol 0mg Carbohydrate 12.2g Fiber 4.1g

35. Garlic Spinach

Preparation Time: 5 minutes

Cooking Time: 5 minutes

Servings: 2

Ingredients:

- ½ tablespoon unsalted butter
- 1 tablespoon garlic powder
- 2 cups fresh spinach

- ¼ teaspoon salt
- ½ lemon, juiced

Directions:

1. Select Sauté on the Instant Pot. When the pot is hot, add butter.

2. Stir in the garlic powder; cook and stir until the garlic is fragrant, about 30 seconds.

3. Add the spinach a few handfuls at a time, secure the lid on the pot.

4. Close the pressure-release valve. Select Manual and set the pot at High Pressure for 5 minutes.

5. At the end of the cooking time, allow the pot to sit undisturbed for 10 minutes, then release any remaining pressure, stir in the lemon juice, and season with salt.

Nutrition: Calories 51 Fat 3.1g Cholesterol 8mg Carbohydrate 5.5g Fiber 1.5g

36. Green Curry Mushrooms

Preparation Time: 15 minutes

Cooking Time: 10 minutes

Servings: 2

Ingredients:

- 1 ½ cups water
- 1 1/2 tablespoons vegetable oil
- 1 cup mushrooms, drained and cubed
- ¼ teaspoon salt
- 1 cup soy milk
- 1 tablespoon green curry paste

Directions:

1. Select Sauté on the Instant Pot. When the Instant Pot is hot, add vegetable oil. Stir in mushrooms. Stirring occasionally, fry about 5 minutes, until evenly crisp and lightly browned. Season with salt.

2. Add soy milk green curry paste.

3. Secure the lid on the pot. Close the pressure-release valve. Select Manual and set the pot at High Pressure for 5 minutes. At the end of the cooking time, allow the pot to sit undisturbed for 10 minutes, then release any remaining pressure.

Nutrition: Calories 237 Fat 15.7g Cholesterol 0mg Carbohydrate 12.1g Fiber 1.9g

37. Onion Millet

Preparation Time: 5 minutes

Cooking Time: 20 minutes

Servings: 2

Ingredients:

- ½ tablespoon vegetable oil
- 1 red onion, chopped
- ½ cup millet
- ½ teaspoon ground black pepper
- 1 cup vegetable broth

Directions:

1. Heat the oil in an Instant Pot on Sauté mode. Stir in the onion, and cook until almost tender. Stir in millet and continue cooking until coated with oil. When the onion is tender, and millet begins to brown lightly, season with pepper, and pour in the vegetable broth. Close Instant Pot with the pressure valve to Sealing. Cook on Manual for 10 minutes followed by 10-minute natural pressure release.

2. Open Instant Pot.

3. Enjoy.

Nutrition: Calories 262 Fat 6.3g Cholesterol 0mg Carbohydrate 42.4g Fiber 5.6g

38. Mango-Lime Rice

Preparation Time: 5 minutes

Cooking Time: 10 minutes

Servings: 2

Ingredients:

- ½ cup brown rice
- 1 cup water
- ¼ tablespoon fresh lime juice
- 1/8 cup chopped fresh rosemary
- ¼ mango, peeled, pitted, and cut into 1/2 inch cubes

Directions:

1. Combine water, brown rice, and lime juice, mango in an Instant Pot.

2. Close the pressure-release valve. Select Manual and set the pot at High Pressure for 10 minutes. At the end of the cooking time, allow the pot to sit undisturbed for 10 minutes, then release any remaining pressure.

3. Serve with fresh rosemary.

4. Enjoy.

Nutrition: Calories 210 Fat 2g Cholesterol 0mg Carbohydrate 45.2g Fiber 3.9g

39. Barley Breakfast Bowl

Preparation Time: 5 minutes

Cooking Time: 30 minutes

Servings: 6

Ingredients: 1½ cups pearl barley

- 3¼ cups water - Large pinch salt
- 1½ cups dried cranberries or cherries
- 3 cups sweetened vanilla plant-based milk
- 2 tablespoons slivered almonds (optional)

Directions:

1. In a large saucepan over high heat, combine the barley, water, and salt. Bring to a boil. Cover the pot, reduce the heat to low, and simmer for 25 to 30 minutes, stirring occasionally, until the water is absorbed.

2. Divide the barley into 6 jars or single-serving storage containers. Add ¼ cup of dried cranberries to each. Pour ½ cup of plant-based milk into each. Add 1 teaspoon of slivered almonds (if using) to each. Close the jars tightly with lids.

Nutrition: Calories 249 Fat 2g Cholesterol 0mg Carbohydrate 54g Fiber 9g

40. Pumpkin Steel-Cut Oats

Preparation Time: 2 minutes

Cooking Time: 35 minutes

Servings: 4

Ingredients:

- 3 cups water - 1 cup steel-cut oats
- ½ cup canned pumpkin purée
- ¼ cup pumpkin seeds (pepitas)
- 2 tablespoons maple syrup
- Pinch salt

Directions:

1. In a large saucepan, bring the water to a boil.

2. Add the oats, stir, and reduce the heat to low. Simmer until the oats are soft, 20 to 30 minutes, continuing to stir occasionally.

3. Stir in the pumpkin purée and continue cooking on low for 3 to 5 minutes longer. Stir in the pumpkin seeds and maple syrup, and season with the salt.

4. Divide the oatmeal into 4 single-serving containers. Let cool before sealing the lids.

Nutrition: Calories 121 Fat 5g Carbohydrate 17g Fiber 2g

41. Amazing Blueberry Smoothie

Preparation Time: 5 minutes

Cooking Time: 0 minutes

Servings: 1

Ingredients:

- ½ avocado
- 1 cup of frozen blueberries
- 1 cup of raw spinach
- Pinch of sea salt
- 1 cup of soy or unsweetened almond milk
- 1 frozen banana

Directions:

1. Blend everything in a powerful blender until you have a smooth, creamy shake. Enjoy your healthy shake and start your morning on a fresh note!

Nutrition: Fat 9 g Carbohydrates 32 g Protein 5 g Calories: 220

42. Perfect Breakfast Shake

Preparation Time: 5 minutes

Cooking Time: 0 minutes

Servings: 1

Ingredients:

- 3 tablespoons of raw cacao powder
- 1 cup of soy/almond milk
- 2 frozen bananas
- 3 tablespoons of natural peanut butter

Directions:

1. Use a powerful blender to combine all the ingredients. Process everything until you have a smooth shake.

2. Enjoy a hearty shake to kick start your day.

Nutrition: Calories: 330 Fat 15 g Carbohydrates 41 g Protein 11 g

43. Go-Green Smoothie

Preparation Time: 5 minutes

Cooking Time: 0 minutes

Servings: 1

Ingredients:

- 2 tablespoons of natural cashew butter

- 1 ripe frozen banana
- 2/3 cup of unsweetened coconut, soy, or almond milk
- 1 large handful of kale or spinach

Directions:

1. Put everything inside a powerful blender.

2. Blend until you have a smooth, creamy shake.

3. Enjoy your special green smoothie.

Nutrition: Calories: 390 Fat19 g Carbohydrates 42 g Protein15 g

44. Amazing Almond & Banana Granola

Preparation Time: 5 minutes

Cooking Time: 70 minutes

Servings: 16

Ingredients:

- 2 peeled and chopped ripe bananas
- 8 cups of rolled oats
- 1 teaspoon of salt
- 2 cups of freshly pitted and chopped dates
- 1 cup of slivered and toasted almonds
- 1 teaspoon of almond extract

Directions:

1. Preheat the oven to 275o F.

2. Put a 13 x 18-inch baking sheets with parchment paper.

3. In a medium saucepan, add 1 cup of water and the dates, and bring to a boil. On medium heat, cook them for

about 10 minutes. The dates will be soft and pulpy. Keep on adding water to the saucepan so that the dates do not stick to the pan.

4. After removing the dates from the heat, allow them to cool before you blend them with salt, almond extract, and bananas.

5. You will have a smooth and creamy puree.

6. Add this mixture to the oats and give it a thorough mix.

7. Divide the mixture into equal halves and spread over the baking sheets.

8. In your preheated oven, bake it for about 30-40 minutes, stirring every 10 minutes or so.

9. So that you will notice that granola is ready when it becomes crispy.

10. After removing the baking sheets from the oven, allow them to cool. Then add the slivered almonds.

11. You can store your granola in an airtight container and enjoy it whenever you are hungry.

Nutrition: Calories: 248.9 Fat 9.4 g Carbohydrate 35.9 g Protein 7.6 g

45. <u>Perfect Polenta with a Dose of Cranberries & Pears</u>

Preparation Time: 5 minutes

Cooking Time: 100 minutes

Servings: 4

Ingredients:

- 2 pears freshly cored, peeled, and diced

- 1 batch of warm basic polenta

- ¼ cup of brown rice syrup

- 1 teaspoon of ground cinnamon

- 1 cup of dried or fresh cranberries

Directions:

1. Warm the polenta in a medium-sized saucepan. Then add the cranberries, pears, and cinnamon powder.

2. Cook everything, stirring occasionally. You will know that the dish is ready when the pears are soft.

3. The entire dish will be done within 10 minutes.

4. Divide the polenta equally among 4 bowls. Add some pear compote as the last finishing touch.

5. Now you can dig into this hassle-free breakfast bowl full of goodness.

Nutrition: Calories: 185 Fat 4.6 g Protein 5 g Carbohydrate 6.1 g

46. <u>Tempeh Bacon Smoked to Perfection</u>

Preparation Time: 5 minutes

Cooking Time: 40 minutes

Servings: 10

Ingredients:

- 3 tablespoons of maple syrup

- 8-ounce packages of tempeh

- ¼ cup of soy or tamari sauce

- 2 teaspoons of liquid smoke

Directions:

1. In a steamer basket, steam the block of tempeh.

2. Put the tamari, maple syrup, and liquid smoke in a medium-sized bowl.

3. Once the tempeh cools down, slice into strips and add to the prepared marinade. Remember: the longer the tempeh marinates, the better the flavor will be. If possible, refrigerate overnight. If not, marinate for at least half an hour.

4. In a sauté pan, cook the tempeh on medium-high heat with a bit of the marinade.

5. Once the strips get crispy on one side, turn them over so that both sides are evenly cooked.

6. You can add some more marinade to cook the tempeh, but they should be properly caramelized. It will take about 5 minutes for each side to cook.

7. Enjoy the crispy caramelized tempeh with your favorite dip.

Nutrition: Calories: 130 Carbohydrate 17 g Protein 12 g Fat 1 g

47. Vegan Muffins Breakfast Sandwich

Preparation Time: 10 minutes

Cooking Time: 20 minutes

Servings: 2

Ingredients:

- Romesco Sauce: 3-4 tablespoons
- Fresh baby spinach: ½ cup
- Tofu Scramble: 2
- Vegan English muffins: 2
- Avocado: ½ peeled and sliced
- Sliced fresh tomato: 1

Directions:

1. In the oven, toast English muffin

2. Half the muffin and spread romesco sauce

3. Paste spinach to one side, tailed by avocado slices

4. Have warm tofu followed by a tomato slice

5. Place the other muffin half onto the preceding one

Nutrition: Carbs: 18g Protein: 12g Fats: 14g Calories: 276

48. Toasted Rye with Pumpkin Seed Butter

Preparation Time: 10 minutes

Cooking Time: 25 minutes and the cooling time

Servings: 4

Ingredients:

- Pumpkin seeds: 220g
- Date nectar: 1 tsp.
- Avocado oil: 2 tbsp.
- Rye bread: 4 slices toasted

Directions:

1. Toast the pumpkin seed on a frying pan on low heat for 5-7 minutes and stir in between

2. Let them turn golden and remove them from the pan

3. Add to the blender when they cool down and make fine powder

4. Add in avocado oil and salt and then again blend to form a paste

5. Add date nectars too and blend

6. On the toasted rye, spread one tablespoon of this butter and serve with your favorite toppings

Nutrition: Carbs: 3 g Protein: 5 g Fats: 10.3 g Calories: 127

49. Overnight Oats

Preparation Time: 15 minutes

Cooking Time: 15 minutes plus overnight

Servings: 6

Ingredients:

- A pinch of Cinnamon
- 4 cups Almond milk
- 2 ½ cups Porridge oats
- 1 tbsp. Maple syrup
- 1 tbsp. Pumpkin seeds
- 1 tbsp. Chia seeds

Directions:

1. Add all the ingredients to the bowl and combine well

2. Cover the bowl and place it in the fridge overnight

3. Pour more milk in the morning

4. Serve with your favorite toppings

Nutrition Carbs: 32.3 g Protein: 10.2 g Fats: 12.7 g Calories: 298

50. Chickpeas Spread Sourdough Toast

Preparation Time: 15 minutes

Cooking Time: 15 minutes

Servings: 4

Ingredients

- 1 cup rinsed and drained chickpeas
- 1 cup pumpkin puree
- ½ cup vegan yogurt:
- Salt
- 4 slices toasted sourdough

Directions:

1. In a bowl add chickpeas and pumpkin puree and mash using a potato masher

2. Add in salt and yogurt and mix

3. Spread it on a toast and serve

Nutrition Carbs: 33.7g Protein: 8.45g Fats: 2.5g Calories: 187

CHAPTER 2:

LUNCH RECIPES

51. Tomato Soup

Preparation Time: 10 minutes

Cooking Time: 8 hours

Servings: 6

Ingredients:

- 1 cup frozen mirepoix
- ⅓ Cup all-purpose flour
- 1 (28-ounce) can crushed tomatoes
- 1 (6-ounce) can tomato paste
- 1 tablespoon dried basil
- 1 teaspoon dried oregano
- 1 teaspoon salt, plus more for seasoning
- 4 cups chicken or vegetable broth
- 1 bay leaf
- 1 cup milk, warmed
- 2 tablespoons unsalted butter
- Freshly ground black pepper
- ⅔ Cup grated Parmesan cheese

Directions:

1. Combine the mirepoix, flour, crushed tomatoes, tomato paste, basil, oregano, and salt in the slow cooker. Whisk to stir your flour into the tomatoes to incorporate. Add the broth and stir. Add the bay leaf.

2. Cover your slow cooker for it to cook for 8 hours on low.

3. Discard the bay leaf. Stir in the warm milk and butter until the butter is melted. Season with salt and pepper, if needed.

4. Put the soup into your serving bowls, top each serving with Parmesan cheese, and serve.

Nutrition: Calories: 200 Fat: 8g Cholesterol: 22mg Carbohydrates: 25g Fiber: 6g Protein: 11g

52. Black Bean Soup

Preparation Time: 10 minutes

Cooking Time: 8 hours

Servings: 6

Ingredients:

- 8 ounces dried black beans
- 3½ cups water
- 1 smoked ham hock, rinsed
- 1 bay leaf
- 1 teaspoon dried oregano
- 1 teaspoon ground cumin
- 1 teaspoon garlic powder
- 1 teaspoon salt, plus more for seasoning
- Juice of 1 lime
- 1 (8-ounce) can tomato sauce
- Freshly ground black pepper
- Chopped fresh cilantro for garnish

Directions:

1. Combine the black beans, water, ham hock, bay leaf, oregano, cumin, garlic powder, and salt in your slow cooker.

2. Cover and wait for it to cook on low for 8 hours or until the beans are tender.

3. Discard the bay leaf. Stir in the lime juice and tomato sauce. Season with salt and pepper, if needed.

4. Serve your soup into bowls and garnish with cilantro.

Nutrition: Calories: 237 Total Fat: 7g Cholesterol: 43mg Carbohydrates: 23g Fiber: 6g Protein: 21g

53. French Onion Soup

Preparation Time: 15 minutes

Cooking Time: 8 hours

Servings: 4

Ingredients:

- 3 small yellow onions, cut into thin rings
- ¼ cup olive oil or canola oil
- Pinch salt
- Pinch freshly ground black pepper
- Pinch sugar
- 2 (13.5-ounce) cans beef consommé
- ½ cup water
- 4 slices crusty bread (French bread or a baguette works well)
- 1⅓ cups shredded Gruyère cheese

Directions:

1. Put the onions in the slow cooker. Add the olive oil, salt, pepper, and sugar and stir until the onions are coated.

2. Cover and wait for it to cook on low for 8 hours or until onions are soft and caramelized.

3. Pour in the consommé and water and turn the slow cooker to high. Cook until warmed through, about 10 minutes.

4. Put the top oven rack 6 inches below the broiler. Turn on the broiler.

5. Ladle the soup into four oven-safe bowls and place them on a rimmed baking sheet. Place a bread on top of each serving of soup. Sprinkle ⅓ cup of Gruyère cheese on top of each piece of bread.

6. Broil it for one to two minutes, or until the cheese is melted and starts to brown. Serve immediately.

Nutrition: Calories: 384 Total Fat: 24g Cholesterol: 33mg Sodium: 966mg Carbohydrates: 28g Fiber: 3g Protein: 17g

54. Broccoli Cheddar Soup

Preparation Time: 10 minutes

Cooking Time: 8 hours

Servings: 5

Ingredients:

- 2 cups vegetable broth
- 1 pound Yukon Gold potatoes, peeled
- 1 medium yellow onion, diced
- 2 scallions, minced
- 1 teaspoon garlic powder
- ¼ teaspoon ground thyme
- Salt
- Freshly ground black pepper
- 1 (1-pound) package frozen broccoli florets, thawed and drained

- ½ cup shredded extra-sharp Cheddar cheese
- ½ cup milk
- 1 tablespoon unsalted butter

Directions:

1. Combine the broth, potatoes, onion, scallions, garlic powder, and thyme in the slow cooker. Season with salt and pepper.

2. Cover and wait for it to cook on low for 8 hours.

3. Carefully transfer the contents of the slow cooker to a blender in batches if necessary. Purée until smooth, making sure to vent the blender lid for steam. Add three-quarters of the broccoli. Pulse three or four times. Then wait to get the consistency of the soup that you desired.

4. Pour the soup back into the slow cooker. Add the Cheddar, milk, butter, and remaining broccoli and stir. Season with salt and pepper, if needed.

5. Cook until warmed through. Serve.

Nutrition: Calories: 194 Total Fat: 8g Cholesterol: 20mg Sodium: 431mg Total Carbohydrates: 24g Fiber: 5g Protein: 10g

55. Creamy Cauliflower-Broccoli Soup

Preparation Time: 10 minutes

Cooking Time: 8 hours

Servings: 6

Ingredients:

- 2 pounds cauliflower florets
- 2 scallions, minced
- 2 cups vegetable broth
- 1 teaspoon onion powder
- 1 teaspoon garlic powder
- ¼ teaspoon dried thyme
- ½ teaspoon salt, plus more for seasoning
- ¼ teaspoon ground black pepper
- 1 (12-ounce) package frozen broccoli florets
- ½ cup grated Parmesan cheese
- ¼ cup heavy cream

Directions:

1. Combine the cauliflower, scallions, broth, onion powder, garlic powder, thyme, salt, and pepper in a slow cooker.

2. Cover and wait for it to cook on low for 8 hours.

3. Carefully transfer the contents of the slow cooker to a blender in batches if necessary. Purée until smooth, making sure to vent the blender lid for steam. Pour the puréed soup back into the slow cooker.

4. Stir in the broccoli, Parmesan cheese, and cream. Cover and set it on high for 10 minutes, or until heated through.

5. Season with salt and pepper, if needed. Serve soup into bowls and then garnish with more Parmesan cheese, if desired.

Directions: Calories: 124 Total Fat: 5g Cholesterol: 14mg Sodium: 642mg Carbohydrates: 14g Fiber: 6g Protein: 10g

56. Cabbage and Noodles

Preparation Time: 5 minutes

Cooking Time: 5 minutes

Servings: 2

Ingredients: 1 cup wide egg noodles

- 1 1/2 tablespoon butter
- 1 small onion
- 1/2 head green cabbage, shredded
- Salt and pepper to taste

Directions:

1. Add egg noodles, butter, water, onion, green cabbage, pepper, and salt to Instant Pot. Place lid on Instant Pot and lock into place to seal. Pressure Cook on High Pressure for 4 minutes. Use Quick Pressure Release.

2. Serve and enjoy.

Nutrition: Calories 183 Fat 6.8g Cholesterol 31mg Carbohydrate 27.2g Fiber 5.9g

57. Japanese Sushi Rice

Preparation Time: 5 minutes

Cooking Time: 20 minutes

Servings: 2

Ingredients:

- 2 cups water

- 1 teaspoon salt
- 1 teaspoon honey
- ½ sheet nori
- 1 cup uncooked white rice (sushi rice)

Directions:

1. In an Instant Pot, combine the water, salt, honey, and nori. Bring to a boil and add the rice.

2. Close the pressure-release valve. Select Manual and set the pot at High Pressure for 10 minutes. At the end of the cooking time, allow the pot to sit undisturbed for 10 minutes, then release any remaining pressure.

3. Serve and enjoy.

Nutrition: Calories 340 Fat 0.6g Cholesterol 0mg Carbohydrate 76.8g Fiber 1.5g

58. Lemon Mozzarella Pasta

Preparation Time: 5 minutes

Cooking Time: 10 minutes

Servings: 2

Ingredients:

- 4 oz. macaroni
- ¼ cup peas
- ½ cup mozzarella cheese
- ½ tablespoon olive oil
- 1 lemon
- Salt and pepper

Directions:

1. Set Instant Pot to Sauté. Add the olive oil and allow it to sizzle. Add

macaroni, peas, lemon, salt, and pepper.

2. Lock lid. Set pressure cook on high pressure for 10 minutes. When cooking time ends, release pressure and wait for steam to completely stop before opening the lid.

3. Add mozzarella cheese and Stir until everything is combined and coated with sauce.

4. Enjoy.

Nutrition: Calories 273 Fat 5.9g Carbohydrate 46.6g Protein 10.3g

59. Zucchini Noodles

Preparation Time: 10 minutes

Cooking Time: 15 minutes

Servings: 2

Ingredients:

- 2 zucchini, peeled
- Marinara sauce of your choice
- Any other seasonings you wish to use

Directions:

1. Peel & spiralizer your zucchini into noodles.

2. Add some of your favorite sauce to Instant Pot, hit "Sauté" and "Adjust," so it's on the "More" or "High" setting.

3. Once the sauce is boiling, add now the noodles to the pot. Toss the noodles in the sauce and allow them to heat up and soften for a few minutes for about 2-5 minutes.

4. Serve in the bowls and top with grated parmesan, if desired.

5. Enjoy!

Nutrition: Calories 86 Fat 2g Cholesterol 1mg Carbohydrate 15.2g Fiber 3.8g

60. Mexican Beans

Preparation Time: 15 minutes

Cooking Time: 35 minutes

Servings: 2

Ingredients:

- ½ cup dried pinto beans
- 2 cups water
- 1 small onion, chopped
- 1 medium ripe tomato, chopped
- 1 fresh bell pepper, chopped
- 1 tablespoon fresh cilantro, chopped

Directions:

1. Select the High Sauté setting on the Instant Pot, add pinto beans, water, onion, ripe tomato, and bell pepper. Secure the lid. Press the Cancel button to reset the program, then select the Pressure Cook or Manual setting and set the cooking time for 35 minutes at High Pressure.

2. Let the pressure release naturally; this will take 10 to 20 minutes.

3. Garnish with fresh cilantro.

Nutrition: Calories 212 Fat 0.9g Cholesterol 0mg Carbohydrate 40.4g Fiber 9.8g

61. Lime-Mint Soup

Preparation Time: 5 minutes

Cooking Time: 30 minutes

Servings: 4

Ingredients:

- 4 cups vegetable broth
- ¼ cup fresh mint leaves,
- ¼ cup chopped scallions
- 3 garlic cloves
- 3 tablespoons freshly squeezed lime juice

Directions:

1. In a large stockpot, combine the broth, mint, scallions, garlic, and lime juice. Bring to a boil over medium-high heat.

2. Cover the pot and reduce the heat to low. Let it simmer for 15 minutes and serve.

Nutrition: Calories: 55 Fat: 2g Carbohydrates: 5g Fiber: 1g Protein: 5g

62. Lemony Kale Salad

Preparation Time: 10 minutes

Cooking Time: 30 minutes

Servings: 4

Ingredients:

- 2 tablespoons freshly squeezed lemon juice
- ½ tablespoon maple syrup
- 1 teaspoon minced garlic
- 5 cups chopped kale

Directions:

1. Add the lemon juice, maple syrup, and garlic together in a large bowl. Add the kale, massage it in the dressing for 1 to 2 minutes, and serve.

2. Preparation Tip: Make sure to thoroughly massage the kale with the dressing ingredients. This will give the kale a beautiful texture and get the lemon and garlic flavors properly incorporated.

Nutrition: Calories: 51 Fat: 0g Carbohydrates: 11g Fiber: 1g

63. Sautéed Collard Greens

Preparation Time: 10 minutes

Cooking Time: 25 minutes

Servings: 4

Ingredients:

- 1½ pounds collard greens
- 1 cup vegetable broth
- ½ teaspoon garlic powder
- ½ teaspoon onion powder
- ⅛ teaspoon freshly ground black pepper

Directions:

1. Remove the hard middle stems from the greens, then roughly chop the leaves into 2-inch pieces.

2. In a large saucepan, mix together the vegetable broth, garlic powder, onion powder, and pepper. Bring to a boil over medium-high heat, then add the chopped greens. Reduce the heat to low and cover.

3. Cook for 20 minutes, stirring well every 4 to 5 minutes, and serve.

Nutrition: Calories: 28 Total fat: 1g Carbohydrates: 4g Fiber: 2g Protein: 3g

64. French Fries

Preparation Time: 10 minutes

Cooking Time: 60 minutes

Servings: 6

Ingredients:

- 2 pounds medium white potatoes
- 1 to 2 tablespoons no-salt seasoning

Directions:

1. Preheat the oven to 400°F. Line a baking sheet with parchment paper.

2. Wash and scrub potatoes and place them on the baking sheet and bake for 45 minutes.

3. Remove potatoes from the oven. Allow to cool in the refrigerator for about 30 minutes, or until you're ready to make a batch of fries.

4. Preheat the oven to 425°F. Line a baking sheet with parchment paper.

5. Slice the cooled potatoes into the shape of wedges or fries, then toss them in a large bowl with the no-salt seasoning.

6. Spread the coated fries out in an even layer on the baking sheet. Bake for about 7 minutes, then remove from the oven, flip the fries over, and redistribute them in an even layer. Bake again for another 8 minutes, or until the fries are crisp and golden brown, and serve.

Nutrition: Calories: 104 Total fat: 0g Carbohydrates: 24g Fiber: 4g Protein: 3g

65. Easy Vegan Pizza Bread

Preparation Time: 5 minutes

Cooking Time: 20 minutes

Servings: 4

Ingredients:

- 1 whole-wheat loaf, unsliced
- 1 cup Easy One-Pot Vegan Marinara
- 1 teaspoon nutritional yeast
- ½ teaspoon onion powder
- ½ teaspoon garlic powder

Directions:

1. Preheat the oven to 375°F.

2. Halve the loaf of bread lengthwise. Evenly spread the marinara onto each slice of bread, then sprinkle on the nutritional yeast, onion powder, and garlic powder.

3. Place bread on a baking sheet. Bake for 20 minutes, or until the bread is a light golden brown.

Nutrition: Calories: 230 Total fat: 3g Carbohydrates: 38g Fiber: 7g Protein: 13g

66. Baked Mac and Peas

Preparation Time: 15 minutes

Cooking Time: 40 minutes

Servings: 8

Ingredients:

- 1 (16-ounce) package whole-wheat macaroni pasta

- 1 recipe Anytime "Cheese" Sauce
- 2 cups green peas (fresh or frozen)

Directions:

1. Preheat the oven to 400°F.
2. In a large stockpot, cook the pasta per the package instructions for al dente. Drain the pasta.
3. Combine the pasta, sauce, and peas, and mix well in a large baking dish.
4. Bake for 30 minutes, or until the top of the dish turns golden brown.

Nutrition: Calories: 209 Total fat: 3g Carbohydrates: 42g Fiber: 7g Protein: 12g

67. Savory Sweet Potato Casserole

Preparation Time: 15 minutes

Cooking Time: 30 minutes

Servings: 6

Ingredients:

- 8 sweet potatoes, cooked
- ½ cup vegetable broth
- 1 tablespoon dried sage
- 1 teaspoon dried thyme
- 1 teaspoon dried rosemary

Directions:

1. Preheat the oven to 375°F.
2. Peel the cooked sweet potatoes and put them in a baking dish. Mash sweet potatoes using a fork or potato masher. Then mix it in the broth, sage, thyme, and rosemary.

3. Bake for 30 minutes and serve.

Nutrition: Calories: 154 Total fat: 0g Carbohydrates: 35g Fiber: 6g Protein: 3g

68. White Bean and Chickpea Hummus

Preparation Time: 5 minutes

Cooking Time: 30 minutes

Servings: 8

Ingredients:

- 1 (15-ounce) can chickpeas
- 1 (15-ounce) can white beans (cannellini or great northern)
- 3 tablespoons freshly squeezed lemon juice
- 2 teaspoons garlic powder
- 1 teaspoon onion powder

Directions:

1. Prepare the chickpeas and white beans. Make sure to drain and rinse.
2. In a food processor or blender, combine the chickpeas, beans, lemon juice, garlic powder, and onion powder. Process for 1 to 2 minutes, or until the texture is smooth and creamy.
3. Serve right away, or store in a refrigerator-safe container for up to 5 days.

Nutrition: Calories: 69 Total fat: 1g Carbohydrates: 12g Fiber: 4g Protein: 4g

69. Roasted Jalapeño and Lime Guacamole

Preparation Time: 5 minutes

Cooking Time: 10 minutes

Servings: 4

Ingredients:

- 1 to 3 jalapeños (depending on your preferred level of spiciness)
- 1 avocado, peeled and pitted
- 1 tablespoon freshly squeezed lime juice

Directions:

1. Preheat the oven to 400°F. Line a baking sheet with parchment paper.

2. Place the jalapeños on the baking sheet and roast for 8 minutes. (The jalapeño can also be roasted on a grill for 5 minutes if you already have it fired up.)

3. Slice the jalapeños and remove the seeds. Cut the top stem and dice into ⅛-inch pieces. Wash your hands immediately after handling the jalapeños.

4. Use a fork or a masher to mash together the avocado, jalapeño pieces, and lime juice and in a medium bowl. Mash and mix until the guacamole has the preferred consistency. Then serve and enjoy!

Nutrition: Calories: 77 Total fat: 7g Carbohydrates: 5g Fiber: 3g Protein: 1g

70. Avo-Tomato-Pasta

Preparation Time: 5 minutes

Cooking Time: 10 minutes

Servings: 4

Ingredients:

- 7 oz. pasta
- 1 diced avocado
- 14 oz. cherry tomatoes halved or quartered
- 4 tbsp. vinaigrette
- 1 clove garlic 7

Directions:

1. Cook pasta base on the instructions of the packaging. Add the garlic to infuse the taste.

2. Drain the pasta slowly and remove the garlic. In a bowl, mix the avocado and tomatoes, and lightly toss in the vinaigrette. Mash the garlic and add it to the avocado mixture.

3. Drizzle a little olive oil all over the pasta. Mix the avocado mixture into the pasta and serve immediately.

Nutrition: Calories: 371 Total fat: 51g Carbohydrates: 11g Fiber: 16g

71. Braised Cabbage

Preparation Time: 10 minutes

Cooking Time: 10 minutes

Servings: 3

Ingredients:

- 14 oz. chopped cabbage
- 1 onion cut into rings

- 2 peeled and diced tomatoes
- Olive oil for cooking

Directions:

1. Put olive oil in a frying pan and turn it over medium heat. Sauté the onion rings for 3 minutes until soft and starting to brown.

2. Add the tomatoes and braise for another 3 minutes. Reduce the heat and add the cabbage. Stir fry for another 4 minutes until the cabbage softens.

3. Serve while still warm.

Nutrition: Calories: 90 Total fat: 20g Carbohydrates: 1g Fiber: 1g

72. Pesto Pearled Barley

Preparation Time: 2 minutes

Cooking Time: 50 minutes

Servings: 4

Ingredients:

- 1 cup dried barley
- 2½ cups vegetable broth
- ½ cup Parm-y Kale Pesto

Directions:

1. In a medium saucepan, combine the barley and broth and bring to a boil. Cover, reduce the heat to low, and simmer for about 45 minutes, until tender. Remove from the stove and let stand for 5 minutes.

2. Fluff the barley, then gently fold in the pesto.

3. Scoop about ¾ cup into each of 4 single-compartment storage containers. Let cool before sealing the lids.

Nutrition: Calories: 237 Total fat: 6g Carbohydrates: 40g Fiber: 11g

73. Five-Spice Farro

Preparation Time: 3 minutes

Cooking Time: 35 minutes

Servings: 4

Ingredients:

- 1 cup dried faro, rinsed and drained
- 1 teaspoon five-spice powder

Directions:

1. In a medium pot, combine the farro, five-spice powder, and enough water to cover. Bring to a boil; reduce the heat to medium-low, and simmer for 30 minutes. Drain off any excess water. Transfer to a large storage container, or scoop 1 cup farro into each of 4 storage containers. Let cool before sealing the lids.

Nutrition: Calories: 73 Total fat: 0g Carbohydrates: 15g Fiber: 1g

74. Sushi-Style Quinoa

Preparation Time: 2 minutes

Cooking Time: 25 minutes

Servings: 4

Ingredients:

- 2 cups water
- 1 cup dry quinoa, rinsed
- ¼ cup unseasoned rice vinegar
- ¼ cup mirin or white wine vinegar

Directions:

1. In a large saucepan, bring the water to a boil.

2. Add the quinoa to the boiling water, stir, cover, and reduce the heat to low. Simmer for 15 to 20 minutes until the liquid is absorbed. Remove from the heat and let stand for 5 minutes. Fluff with a fork. Add the vinegar and mirin, and stir to combine well.

3. Divide the quinoa evenly among 4 mason jars or single-serving containers. Let cool before sealing the lids.

Nutrition: Calories: 192 Total fat: 3g Carbohydrates: 34g Fiber: 3g

75. Steamed Cauliflower

Preparation Time: 5 minutes

Cooking Time: 10 minutes

Servings: 4

Ingredients:

- 1 large head cauliflower

- 1 cup water

- ½ teaspoon salt

- 1 teaspoon red pepper flakes (optional)

Directions:

1. Remove any leaves from the cauliflower and cut it into florets.

2. In a large saucepan, bring the water to a boil. Place a steamer basket over the water and add the florets and salt. Cover and steam for 5 to 7 minutes, until tender.

3. In a large bowl, toss the cauliflower with the red pepper flakes (if using).

4. Transfer the florets to a large airtight container or 6 single-serving containers. Let cool before sealing the lids.

Nutrition: Calories: 35 Total fat: 0g Carbohydrates: 7g Fiber: 4g

76. Mashed Potatoes and Kale with White Beans

Preparation Time: 10 minutes

Cooking Time: 30 minutes

Servings: 4

Ingredients:

- 2 large Russet potatoes

- Pinch salt (optional), plus ½ teaspoon

- ½ cup vegetable broth

- 6 ounces kale, torn into bite-size pieces

- 1 (14.5-ounce) can great northern beans or other white beans, rinsed and drained

- ¼ to ½ teaspoon freshly ground black pepper, to taste

Directions:

1. Wash (but don't peel!) the potatoes, quarter them, then halve each quarter. Place in a large pot and cover with water. Add a pinch of salt (if using) and bring to a boil. Cover, reduce the heat to medium, and cook for about 20 minutes until the potatoes are tender.

2. Drain the potatoes and return to the pot. Pour the vegetable broth over the potatoes. Add the kale and then the beans. Cover and cook on low heat for about 5 minutes, until the kale turns bright green and is lightly wilted.

3. Use a potato masher to mash everything together, and season with ½ teaspoon salt and pepper.

4. Divide the potatoes, kale, and beans evenly among 4 single-serving containers. Let cool before sealing the lids.

Nutrition: Calories: 255 Total fat: 1g Carbohydrates: 53g Fiber: 11g

.

CHAPTER 3:

MAIN MEALS RECIPES

77. Tempeh Split Pea Burgers

Preparation Time: 10 minutes

Cooking Time: 25 minutes

Servings: 8

Ingredients:

- 3 cups Split peas (cooked or canned)
- 1 14-ounces pack Tempeh
- ½ cup Full-fat coconut milk
- 3 tablespoons Ground flaxseeds
- 3 tablespoons Burger spices

Directions:

1. Cook dry split peas, soak and cook 1 cup (200 g.) of dry split peas according to the procedure in the package.

2. Preheat the oven to 350°F. Line a baking sheet using parchment paper.

3. Add tempeh to the food processor and blend it until a chunky mixture is achieved. Scrape down the sides of the food processor to prevent any lumps.

4. Add the split peas, ground flaxseed, and spices to the food processor and slowly process it along with the tempeh while pouring in the coconut milk to form a chunky mixture.

5. You can also crumble the tempeh by hand in a large bowl, add the remaining ingredients, and mash everything into a chunky mixture.

6. Put every mixture on the baking sheet. Make sure to flatten it into a 1-inch thick. Cut it in square patties making 8 pieces. You can also shape each patty into a circle before baking.

7. Bake the patties for 15 minutes. Take the baking sheet off the oven, then flip the patties. Bake again for another 10 minutes.

8. Take patties out of the oven once the crust is crispy and browned and let them cool down for about a minute.

9. Serve and enjoy!

Nutrition: Calories: 236 Carbs: 18 g. Fat: 9.5 g. Protein: 18.3 g.

78. Crispy Marinated Tempeh

Preparation Time: 15 minutes

Cooking Time: 25 minutes

Servings: 2

Ingredients:

- 1 14-ounces pack Tempeh (cubed)
- ¼ cup Low-sodium soy sauce
- ¼ cup Lemon juice
- 4-inches piece Ginger (minced)
- 4 cloves Garlic (minced)

Directions:

1. Put the tempeh cubes in an airtight with all the other ingredients.

2. Close and shake well until the tempeh cubes are covered evenly with the ingredients.

3. Use an airtight container and put it in the fridge for at least 2 hours or overnight to make sure the tempeh is marinated thoroughly.

4. Preheat oven to 375°F. Line a baking sheet using parchment paper.

5. Transfer tempeh onto the baking sheet, then bake for 25 minutes or

until the tempeh is browned and crispy.

6. Serve the tempeh and enjoy!

Nutrition: Calories: 431 Carbs: 10.5 g. Fat: 19.4 g. Protein: 47.9 g

79. BBQ-LT Sandwich

Preparation Time: 15 minutes

Cooking Time: 15 minutes

Servings: 2

Ingredients:

- 1 7-ounces pack Tempeh (thinly sliced)
- ½ cup BBQ sauce
- 2 large tomatoes (sliced)
- 4 leaves Lettuce
- 4 whole wheat buns

Directions:

1. Add the tempeh slices and the BBQ sauce to an airtight container.

2. Close airtight container, mix well and put it in the fridge. Allow the tempeh to marinate for 1 hour up until 12 hours.

3. Preheat your oven to 375°F. Line a baking sheet u parchment paper.

4. Transfer the tempeh slices onto the baking sheet and bake for about 15 minutes or until the tempeh is browned and crispy.

5. Bake the buns with the tempeh for the last 5 minutes if you want crispy and browned bread.

6. Spread the optional guacamole on the bottom half of each bun and add a lettuce leaf on top,

7. Put a quarter of the BBQ tempeh slices on top of the lettuce on each bun. Top it with 2 slices of tomato per bun.

8. Cover with the top halves of the buns, serve the sandwiches right away, and enjoy!

Nutrition: Calories: 260 Carbs: 14.85 g. Fat: 10 g. Protein: 24 g.

80. Mango Satay Tempeh Bowl

Preparation Time: 15 minutes

Cooking Time: 30 minutes

Servings: 4

Ingredients:

- 1 cup Black beans (cooked or canned)
- ½ cup Quinoa (dry)
- 1 14-ounces pack Tempeh (sliced)
- 1 cup Peanut butter
- 1 cup Mango cubes (frozen or fresh)

Directions:

1. Soak and cook ⅓ cup (56 g.) of dry black beans according to the method and cook the quinoa according to the package instructions.

2. Blend the mango into a smooth puree using a blender or food processor or blender and set it aside.

3. Add the tempeh slices and the peanut butter to an airtight container.

4. Close the lid and shake well until the tempeh slices are evenly covered with the peanut butter.

5. Preheat your oven and set it to 375°F. Line a baking sheet using parchment paper.

6. Transfer the peanut butter tempeh slices to the baking sheet. Bake for15 minutes or until tempeh is browned and crispy.

7. Divide the black beans, quinoa, mango puree, and tempeh slices between two bowls, serve with the optional toppings and enjoy!

Nutrition: Calories: 732 Carbs: 39 g. Fat: 42.2 g. Protein: 46.2 g

81. **Fried Rice with Tofu Scramble**

Preparation Time: 15 minutes

Cooking Time: 35 minutes

Servings: 2

Ingredients:

- 4 cups Quick-cooking brown rice (cooked)

- 1 cup Green peas and Carrots (julienned)

- 1 7-oz pack Extra-firm tofu (scrambled)

- ¼ cup Curry spices

- 1 cup Water

Directions:

1. Cook brown rice according to the instructions.

2. Put the pan over medium heat and add ½ cup of water and the tofu scramble.

3. Add the curry spices and cook for about 5 minutes, stirring occasionally to prevent the tofu from sticking to the pan, until the tofu is well heated and most of the water has evaporated.

4. Add the carrots, rice, and green peas along with the remaining ½ cup water and stir-fry until the water evaporated.

5. Turn off the heat, divide the fried rice between 2 bowls, serve with the optional toppings, and enjoy!

Nutrition: Calories: 285 Carbs: 30.2 g. Fat: 10.2 g. Protein: 18.1 g.

82. **Soy Mince Noodle Bowl**

Preparation Time: 15 minutes

Cooking Time: 15 minutes

Servings: 2

Ingredients:

- 2 packs Brown rice noodles

- 1 7-ounces pack textured soy mince

- 2 yellow onions (minced)

- 4 cloves Garlic (minced)

- ¼ cup Low-sodium soy sauce

- 1½ cups Water

Directions:

1. Cook noodles according to the instructions, then drain the excess water with a strainer and set aside.

2. Put a pot and turn it in a medium heat. Add ½ cup of water, the soy sauce, minced onion, and garlic.

3. Add the soy mince and cook for about 5 minutes, stirring occasionally to prevent the soy mince from sticking to the pan, until the mince has cooked and half of the water has evaporated.

4. Add the remaining water, then bring to boil while stirring occasionally.

5. Turn off the heat, add the noodles, and stir well until everything is evenly mixed.

6. Divide the noodles and mince between 2 bowls, serve with the optional toppings, and enjoy!

Nutrition: Calories: 226 Carbs: 26.3 g. Fat: 0.7 g. Protein: 25.3 g.

83. Sweet Potato Tacos

Preparation Time: 15 minutes

Cooking Time: 5 minutes

Servings: 6

Ingredients:

- 2 cups Black beans (cooked or canned)
- 1 7-oz pack textured soy mince
- 3 small sweet potatoes (cubed)
- 6 whole wheat taco shells
- ¼ cup Mexican chorizo seasoning
- 1 cup Water

Directions:

1. When using dry beans, soak and cook 1½ cup (113 g.) of dry black beans according to the procedure.

2. Put water in a pot, then put cubed potatoes. Make sure to pot is over medium-high heat for 15 minutes or

until cooked. Drain excess water, then set aside the potatoes.

3. Put the pan over medium-high heat. Make sure to use a non-stick pan. Add soy mince, black beans, chorizo seasoning, and a cup of water.

4. Stir continuously until everything is cooked, then add the cooked sweet potato cubes.

5. Turn the heat off, then stir occasionally for 5 minutes until cooked. Divide sweet potato mixture for 6 taco shells.

6. Serve and enjoy!

Nutrition: Calories: 202 Carbs: 29.7 g. Fat: 2.85 g. Protein: 13.2 g.

84. Marinated Mushroom Scramble

Preparation Time: 15 minutes

Cooking Time: 15 minutes

Servings: 4

Ingredients:

- 2 cups Button mushrooms
- 1 14-ounces pack Extra-firm tofu (scrambled)
- 2 medium yellow onions (thinly sliced)
- ¼ cup Low-sodium soy sauce
- ½ cup Tahini
- ½ cup Water

Directions:

1. Add the mushrooms, tofu scramble, and soy sauce to an airtight container. Then close the lid and shake well until

everything is evenly covered with soy sauce.

2. Put the container in the fridge and leave to marinate for at least an hour or up to 12 hours.

3. Put the pan over medium heat. Add the water and tofu mushroom mixture to the pan.

4. Add onion, then cook it for 15 minutes, stirring occasionally with a spatula to prevent the tofu from sticking to the pan, until the mushrooms are cooked, and most of the water has evaporated.

5. Turn the heat off and divide tofu mushroom scramble into 2 bowls.

6. Top the bowls with the tahini, serve with the optional toppings, and enjoy!

7. Store the tofu mushroom scramble in an airtight container in the fridge.

Nutrition: Calories: 340 Carbs: 12.6 g. Fat: 23.3 g. Protein: 20 g.

85. Mac 'N' Mince

Preparation Time: 15 minutes

Cooking Time: 10 minutes

Servings: 4

Ingredients:

- 2 cups Whole wheat macaroni
- 7-ounces pack textured soy mince
- ½ cup Tahini
- ¼ cup Nutritional yeast
- 2 tablespoons Lemon garlic pepper seasoning
- ½ cup Water

Directions:

1. Cook the macaroni according to instructions and then set it aside afterward.

2. Put a frying pan over medium-high heat. Make sure to use a non-stick pan, then add the soy mince together with the ¼ cup water.

3. Stir fry soy mince until cooked and make sure most of the water evaporated.

4. Then add the ¼ cup of water, nutritional yeast, lemon garlic pepper seasoning, tahini, and then put turmeric to the soy mince, but this is optional.

5. Cook a little longer until well combined.

6. Add the cooked macaroni to the pan with soy mince. Stir this thoroughly until mixed well.

7. Divide mac 'n' mince into two plates. Serve and enjoy!

Nutrition: Calories: 454 Carbs: 42 g. Fat: 19.9 g. Protein: 25.05 g

86. Moroccan Chickpea Rolls

Preparation Time: 10 minutes

Cooking Time: 25 minutes

Servings: 6

Ingredients:

- 5 cups Chickpeas (cooked or canned)
- ¼ cup full-flat coconut milk
- ¼ copra's El Han out

Directions:

1. Now with the chickpeas, soak, then cook 1½ cup of dry chickpeas according to the procedure if necessary.

2. Prepare oven, then preheat it to 350°F/175°C, then line a baking sheet using the parchment paper.

3. Add chickpeas and other spices to the food processor. Slowly pour in the coconut milk to form a chunky mixture.

4. Mash chickpeas and spices in a large bowl and then add the coconut milk and knead everything into a chunky mixture.

5. Get a handful of chickpea mixture, then knead into a log shape, make sure it is 4 inches long and also 2 inches thick.

6. Make until you have 16 rolls in totality.

7. Place the rolled chickpeas on the baking sheet, and bake for 15 minutes.

8. Get the baking sheet off the oven and turn the rolls over, then bake for another 10 minutes.

9. Take the rolls out of the oven once cooked. Make sure it is brown and crispy. Let it cool down.

10. Serve the rolls with the optional toppings.

Nutrition: Calories: 490 Carbs: 75.3 g. Fat: 10.3 g. Protein: 24 g.

87. Smoky Cajun Bowl

Preparation Time: 10 minutes

Cooking Time: 25 minutes

Servings: 4

Ingredients:

- 2 cups Black beans (cooked or canned)
- 1 cup Quick-cooking brown rice (dry)
- 1 7-ounces pack Smoked tofu (cubed)
- 2 cups Tomato cubes (canned or fresh)
- 1 tablespoon Salt-free Cajun spices

Directions:

1. When using dry beans, make sure to soak and cook ⅔ cup (113 g.) of dry black beans according to the procedure. Cook brown rice base and using package instructions.

2. Put the pan over medium-high heat. Add tofu cubes, tomato cubes, and you can also add ¼ cup of water.

3. Stir until everything is cooked. Afterward, add the black beans, cooked brown rice, and Cajun spices.

4. Turn heat off, then stir occasionally for 5 minutes until heated through.

5. Then divide the smoky Cajun beans and rice between 4 bowls, serve with the optional toppings, and enjoy

6. Store smoky Cajun beans and rice in an airtight container in the fridge, and you can consume it within 3 days. You can also store for a maximum of 30 days in the fridge and thaw at room temperature. You can use a microwave, toaster oven, or non-stick

frying pan to reheat the smoky Cajun beans and rice.

Nutrition: Calories: 371 Carbs: 60.6 g Fat: 5 g. Protein: 19.6 g.

88. Sloppy Cajun Burgers

Preparation Time: 10 minutes

Cooking Time: 5 minutes

Servings: 4

Ingredients:

- 1 cup Black beans (cooked or canned)
- 1 7-ounces pack textured soy mince
- 1 cup Tomato cubes (canned or fresh)
- ¼ cup Salt-free Cajun spices
- 4 whole wheat buns

Directions:

1. When using dry beans, make sure to soak and cook ⅓ cup (56 g.) of dry black beans according to the method

2. Put the non-stick deep frying pan on medium-high heat and add the soy mince and the tomato cubes.

3. Cook for about 3 minutes and stir occasionally until everything is cooked.

4. Add the black beans and Cajun spices and let it cook for another 2 minutes while stirring.

5. Turn off the heat and divide the bottom halves of the buns between 2 plates.

6. Transfer a quarter of the sloppy Cajun mix onto each of the bun halves and add the optional toppings.

7. Cover each burger with the other bun half, serve right away and enjoy!

8. Store the sloppy Cajun mix in an airtight container in the fridge and consume within 2 days. You can store in the freezer for a maximum of 60 days and thaw at room temperature. The sloppy Cajun mix can be served cold or reheated in a microwave or a saucepan.

Nutrition: Calories: 134 Carbs: 15.8 g. Fat: 0.7 g. Protein: 14.7 g.

89. Spaghetti Bolognese

Preparation Time: 15 minutes

Cooking Time: 5 minutes

Servings: 4

Ingredients:

- 2 cups Whole wheat spaghetti (dry)
- 1 7-ounces pack textured soy mince
- 3 cloves Garlic (minced)
- 1 cup Tomato cubes (canned or fresh)
- ¼ cup Basil (fresh or dried)

Directions:

1. Cook spaghetti according to instructions of its package, drain the water with a strainer, then set it aside.

2. Put a non-stick deep frying pan over medium-high heat and add the soy mince, minced garlic, tomato cubes, and basil.

3. Cook it for about 2 minutes and stir occasionally until everything is cooked.

4. Turn off the heat, the divide the spaghetti between 2 plates, and add half of the sauce on top of the spaghetti on each plate.

5. Serve with the optional toppings and enjoy!

6. Store the spaghetti and sauce in an airtight container in the fridge.

7. You can consume this within 3 days. Also, it can be stored in the freezer for a maximum of 30 days and thaw at room temperature. Use a microwave or a saucepan to reheat the spaghetti and sauce.

Nutrition: Calories: 215 Carbs: 44.4 g Fat: 1.9 g Protein: 18.1 g

90. Black Bean Quinoa Burgers

Preparation Time: 10 minutes

Cooking Time: 35 minutes

Servings: 4

Ingredients:

- 1 cup Quinoa (dry)
- 2 cups Black beans (cooked)
- ¼ cup Mexican chorizo seasoning

Directions:

1. Make sure to soak then cook ⅔ cup (113 g.) of dry black beans according to the procedure.

2. Make sure to preheat oven to 375°F/190°C and line a baking sheet with parchment paper.

3. Add cooked black beans, quinoa, and spices to the food processor. Blend until a chunky mixture, scraping down

the sides of the food processor to prevent any lumps if necessary.

4. You can add ingredients to the bowl, then mash them until it turns into a chunky mixture.

5. Put every mixture on the baking sheet.

6. Make sure to flatten it into a 1-inch-thick square, then cut the square into 8 patties. Shape every in circles.

7. Bake patties for 10 minutes. Take the baking sheet off the oven, then flip the patties. Bake again for another 10 minutes.

8. Get the patties out once they are cooked. Make sure that crust is crispy and browned.

9. Let them cool down and enjoy!

Nutrition: Calories: 282 Carbs: 47.4 g. Fat: 3.4 g. Protein: 14.4 g.

91. Tomato Curry Fritters

Preparation Time: 10 minutes

Cooking Time: 16 minutes

Servings: 6

Ingredients:

- 5 cups Chickpeas (cooked or canned)
- 2 sweet onions (diced)
- 12 sundried tomatoes
- 3 cloves Garlic (minced)
- ¼ cup Curry spices

Directions:

1. If you're using dry chickpeas, make sure to soak and cook 1½ cup (330 g.) of dry chickpeas according to the method.

2. Preheat oven to 375°F/190°C. Place parchment paper on a baking sheet.

3. Put the chickpeas, onion, sundried tomatoes, garlic, and spices to the food processor and process them until it turns chunky mixture.

4. Alternatively, mince the sundried tomatoes, mash them together with the chickpeas and other ingredients in a large bowl, and knead them into a chunky mixture.

5. Take a tablespoon of the chickpea mixture and knead into a 2-inch-thick (5cm) disc, then place on the baking sheet until you make 24 fritters.

6. Afterward, bake the fritters for eight minutes. Take the baking sheet off the oven, turn the fritters over and bake for another 8 minutes.

7. Take fritters out of the oven once cooked. Make sure it is brown and crispy. Let them cool down.

Nutrition: Calories: 173 Carbs: 22 g Fat: 4 g Protein: 13 g Fiber:9.3g Sugar: 9 g

92. Baked Ziti

Preparation Time: 15 minutes

Cooking Time: 20 minutes

Servings: 6

Ingredients:

- 16 oz. vegan ziti pasta

- 15 oz. canned chickpeas

- 2 cups baby spinach

- 4 cups tomato sauce

- 1 ½ cup non-dairy cheese

Directions:

1. Preheat the oven to 400 F.

2. Cook the ziti pasta base on packaging instruction. Strain the pasta and return the pasta to the pot.

3. Add the chickpeas, spinach, and tomato sauce to the pasta and mix well. Pour half the pasta mixture into your oven dish and spread equally. Sprinkle with ¾ cup sugar. Layer the rest of the pasta mixture on top and sprinkle with the remaining cheese.

4. Cover the dish with aluminum foil and bake for 20 minutes.

5. Serve while still warm.

Nutrition: Calories: 405 Carbs: 53g Fat: 11g Protein: 25g

93. Black Bean Veggie Burgers

Preparation Time: 10 minutes

Cooking Time: 20 minutes

Servings: 4

Ingredients:

- 30 oz. canned, drained black beans

- ¾ cup rolled oats

- 1 canned chipotle pepper in adobo chili sauce, as well as 1 tbsp. of the sauce

- 1 avocado

- Olive oil for cooking

Directions:

1. Preheat your oven to 350 F.

2. Rinse your beans and place them on your baking tray. Bake for 10 minutes

until the beans become dry to the touch and start to split.

3. Place the beans in your food processor along with the oats, chipotle pepper, and sauce. Pulse until the ingredients start to stick together. This should take roughly 20 seconds.

4. Mash the avocado in a bowl and add the bean mixture. Stir and fold together until everything forms a dough-like ball. Form the mixture into four balls and flatten them into patties.

5. Heat some olive oil in a frying pan over medium heat. Fry the patties for 3 - 4 minutes on each side.

6. Serve the patties on some whole grain, vegan buns together with all your favorite burger toppings.

Nutrition: Calories: 112 Carbs: 21g Fat: 0g Protein: 7g

94. Tortilla Pizza with Hummus

Preparation Time: 10 minutes

Cooking Time: 17 minutes

Servings: 1

Ingredients:

- 1 - 2 vegan tortilla shells (depending on how hungry you are)
- ⅓ cup hummus per tortilla shell
- Toppings of your choice
- ½ - ¾ cup grated vegan mozzarella per tortilla shell
- Chopped thyme

Directions:

1. Preheat the oven to 400 F.

2. Place the tortilla shells on your baking tray and bake for 7 minutes until golden brown. Remove from the oven and let cool while preparing your toppings. Do not turn off your oven.

3. Spread the hummus over the tortilla shells and add your toppings. Cover with the vegan mozzarella. Sprinkle with a little chopped thyme.

4. Put back into the oven and bake for 10 minutes.

5. Slice the pizza shell and serve immediately.

Nutrition: Calories: 214 Carbs: 16g Fat: 14g Protein: 12g

95. Stir Fry

Preparation Time: 10 minutes

Cooking Time: 15 minutes

Servings: 2

Ingredients:

- 3 cups chopped cabbage
- 1 large roughly chopped onion
- 2 roughly chopped green peppers - the veggies should add up to about 5 cups
- 3 tbsp. Chinese stir fry sauce
- 6 tbsp. water
- Olive oil for cooking

Directions:

1. Place olive oil in a wok over high heat. Sauté the onions for 2 minutes until

soft and transparent. Add the cabbage and green peppers and cook for 7 - 10 minutes until everything is fully cooked.

2. Add the stir fry sauce and water. Toss the veggies lightly to make sure everything is covered.

3. Cook for another minute until the sauce becomes thick and glossy. Serve and enjoy!

Nutrition: Calories: 40 Carbs: 0g Fat: 4g Protein: 25g

96. Spanakorizo

Preparation Time: 5 minutes

Cooking Time: 20 minutes

Servings: 6

Ingredients:

- 1 ½ cup cooked brown rice
- 2 lb. fresh spinach
- 1 cup tomato sauce
- 2 chopped onions
- 1 cup water
- Olive oil for cooking

Directions:

1. Place olive oil in the large pot over high heat. Sauté the onions until soft and slightly transparent.

2. Add the fresh spinach, tomato sauce, and water and bring to a boil. Reduce the heat and add the rice.

3. Cover and let it simmer for 10 minutes.

4. Garnish with some fresh herbs and serve.

Nutrition: Calories: 295 Carbs: 48g Fat: 8g Protein: 10g

97. Roast Chili Lime Chickpeas

Preparation Time: 5 minutes

Cooking Time: 30 minutes

Servings: 2

Ingredients:

- 1 15oz chickpeas, drained and rinsed
- 2 tablespoons olive oil
- 2 teaspoons chili powder
- 1 tablespoon lime zest
- ½ teaspoon salt

Directions:

1. Heat the oven to 400. Dry the drained chickpeas by patting them with a paper towel. Place the chickpeas into a bowl with the olive oil and toss them together well. Bake the chickpeas for thirty minutes on a baking sheet. After they have baked, place them back into the bowl and toss with the salt, lime zest, and chili powder.

Nutrition: Calories: 151 Carbs: 19g Fat: 6g Protein: 6g

98. Avocado Toast

Preparation Time: 5 minutes

Cooking Time: 0 minutes

Servings: 1

Ingredients:

- Salt, one quarter teaspoon

- Black pepper, one half teaspoon
- Avocado, one peeled and sliced thinly
- Whole grain bread, two slices toasted

Directions:

1. Slice the avocado while the bread is toasting. Lay the slices of avocado onto the toast and sprinkle on the pepper and salt.

Nutrition: Calories: 362 Carbs: 30g Fat: 25g Protein: 10g

99. Hemp Porridge with Pears And Blueberries

Preparation Time: 5 minutes

Cooking Time: 5 minutes

Servings: 1

Ingredients:

- Almond milk, one cup
- Blueberries, one half cup
- Hemp seeds, one half tablespoons
- Pear, one medium-sized sliced
- Porridge oats, one half cup

Directions:

1. In a medium-sized saucepan over a medium heat, pour in the porridge and the almond milk. Bring the mix to a boil and then turn down the heat and let the porridge simmer for five minutes. Spoon the porridge into a bowl and top it with the blueberries, hemp seeds, and pears and serve.

Nutrition: Calories: 463 Carbs: 78g Fat: 11g Protein: 17g

100. Basic Baked Potatoes

Preparation Time: 5 minutes

Cooking Time: 60 minutes

Servings: 5

Ingredients:

- 5 medium Russet potatoes or a variety of potatoes, washed and patted dry
- 1 to 2 tablespoons extra-virgin olive oil or aquafaba - ¼ teaspoon salt
- ¼ teaspoon freshly ground black pepper

Directions:

1. Preheat the oven to 400°F.
2. Pierce each potato several times with a fork or a knife. Brush the olive oil over the potatoes, then rub each with a pinch of the salt and a pinch of the pepper. Place the potatoes on a baking sheet and bake for 50 to 60 minutes until tender.
3. Place the potatoes on a baking rack and cool completely. Transfer to an airtight container or 5 single-serving containers. Let cool before sealing the lids.

Nutrition: Calories: 171 Carbs: 34g Fat: 3g Protein: 4g

101. Miso Spaghetti Squash

Preparation Time: 5 minutes

Cooking Time: 40 minutes

Servings: 4

Ingredients:

- 1 (3-pound) spaghetti squash

- 1 tablespoon hot water
- 1 tablespoon unseasoned rice vinegar
- 1 tablespoon white miso

Directions:

1. Preheat the oven to 400°F. Line a rimmed baking sheet with parchment paper.

2. Halve the squash lengthwise and place, cut-side down, on the prepared baking sheet. Bake for 35 to 40 minutes, until tender.

3. Cool until the squash is easy to handle. With a fork, scrape out the flesh, which will be stringy, like spaghetti. Transfer to a large bowl.

4. In a small bowl, combine the hot water, vinegar, and miso with a whisk or fork. Pour over the squash. Gently toss with tongs to coat the squash.

5. Divide the squash evenly among 4 single-serving containers. Let cool before sealing the lids.

Nutrition: Calories: 171 Carbs: 25g Fat: 2g Protein: 3g

CHAPTER 4:

VEGETABLES, SALADS AND SIDES RECIPES

102. Mashed Cauliflower

Preparation Time: 10 minutes

Cooking Time: 15 minutes

Servings: 2

Ingredients:

- 4 cups cauliflower florets
- ¼ cup skim milk
- ¼ cup (2 ounces) grated Parmesan cheese
- 2 tablespoons butter
- 2 tablespoons extra-virgin olive oil

Directions:

- In a large pot over medium-high, cover the cauliflower with water and bring it to a boil.
- Reduce the heat to medium-low, cover, and simmer for about 10 minutes until the cauliflower is soft.
- Drain the cauliflower and return it to the pot. Add the milk, cheese, butter, olive oil, sea salt, and pepper.
- Using a potato masher, mash until smooth.

Nutrition: Calories per Serving: 192; Carbs: 16.1g; Protein: 3.9g; Fats: 13.8g

103. Broccoli with Ginger and Garlic

Preparation Time: 10 minutes

Cooking Time: 11 minutes

Servings: 2

Ingredients:

- 2 tablespoons extra-virgin olive oil

- 2 cups broccoli florets
- 1 tablespoon grated fresh ginger
- 3 garlic cloves, minced

Directions:

- In a large skillet over medium-high heat, heat the olive oil until it shimmers.
- Add the broccoli, ginger, sea salt, and pepper. Cook for about 10 minutes, stirring occasionally, until the broccoli is soft and starts to brown.
- Add the garlic and cook for 30 seconds, stirring constantly. Remove from the heat and serve.

Nutrition:

Calories per Serving: 192;

Carbs: 16.1g;

Protein: 3.9g;

Fats: 13.8g

104. Balsamic Roasted Carrots

Preparation Time: 10 minutes

Cooking Time: 30 minutes

Servings: 2

Ingredients:

- 1½ pounds carrots, quartered lengthwise
- 2 tablespoons extra-virgin olive oil
- ¼ teaspoon sea salt
- 1/8 teaspoon freshly ground black pepper
- 3 tablespoons balsamic vinegar

Directions:

- Preheat the oven to 425°F. In a large bowl, toss the carrots with the olive oil, sea salt, and pepper.

- Place in a single layer in a roasting pan or on a rimmed baking sheet.

- Roast for 20 to 30 minutes until the carrots are caramelized. Toss with the vinegar and serve.

Nutrition:

Calories per Serving: 192;

Carbs: 16.1g;

Protein: 3.9g;

Fats: 13.8g

105.   Chives and Radishes Platter

Preparation Time: 10 minutes

Cooking Time: 7 minutes

Servings: 2

Ingredients

- 2 cups radishes, quartered

- ½ cup vegetable stock

- Salt and pepper to taste

- 2 tablespoons melted ghee

- 1 tablespoon chives, chopped

Direction

- Add radishes, stock, salt, pepper, zest to your Ninja Foodi and stir

- Lock lid and cook on HIGH pressure for 7 minutes

- Quick release pressure. Add melted ghee, toss well. Sprinkle chives and enjoy!

Nutrition:

Calories per Serving: 192;

Carbs: 16.1g;

Protein: 3.9g;

Fats: 13.8g

106.   Healthy Rosemary and Celery Dish

Preparation Time: 10 minutes

Cooking Time: 5 minutes

Servings: 2

Ingredients

- 1-pound celery, cubed

- 1 cup of water

- 2 garlic cloves, minced

- Salt and pepper

- ¼ teaspoon dry rosemary

- 1 tablespoon olive oil

Direction

- Add water to your Ninja Foodi and place steamer basket

- Add celery cubs to basket and lock lid, cook on HIGH pressure for 4 minutes

- Quick release pressure. Take a bowl and add mix in oil, garlic, and rosemary. Whisk well

- Add steamed celery to the bowl and toss well, spread on a lined baking sheet

- Broil for 3 minutes using the Air Crisping lid at 250 degrees F. Serve and enjoy!

Nutrition:

Calories: 190,

Fats: 10g,

Dietary Fiber: 3.1g,

Carbohydrates: 25.5g,

Protein: 3.2g

107. Hearty Cheesy Cauliflower

Preparation Time: 10 minutes

Cooking Time: 35 minutes

Servings: 2

Ingredients

- 1 tablespoon Keto-Friendly mustard
- 1 head cauliflower
- 1 teaspoon avocado mayonnaise
- ½ cup parmesan cheese, grated
- ¼ cup butter, cut into small pieces

Directions

- Set your Ninja Foodi to Sauté mode and add butter, let it melt
- Add cauliflower and Sauté for 3 minutes
- Add rest of the ingredients and lock lid, cook on HIGH pressure for 30 minutes
- Release pressure naturally over 10 minutes. Serve and enjoy!

Nutrition:

Calories: 190,

Fats: 10g,

Dietary Fiber: 3.1g,

Carbohydrates: 25.5g,

Protein: 3.2g

108. Mesmerizing Spinach Quiche

Preparation Time: 10 minutes

Cooking Time: 33 minutes

Servings: 2

Ingredients

- 1 tablespoon butter, melted
- 1 pack (10 ounces) frozen spinach, thawed
- 5 organic eggs, beaten
- Salt and pepper to taste
- 3 cups Monterey Jack Cheese, shredded

Directions

- Set your Ninja Foodi to Sauté mode and let it heat up, add butter and let the butter melt
- Add spinach and Sauté for 3 minutes, transfer the Sautéed spinach to a bowl
- Add eggs, cheese, salt, and pepper to a bowl and mix it well
- Transfer the mixture to greased quiche molds and transfer the mold to your Foodi
- Close the lid and choose the "Bake/Roast" mode and let it cook for 30 minutes at 360 degrees F. Once done, open lid and transfer the dish out

- Cut into wedges and serve. Enjoy!

Nutrition:

Calories per Serving: 192;

Carbs: 16.1g;

Protein: 3.9g;

Fats: 13.8g

109. Simple Mushroom Hats and Eggs

Preparation Time: 10 minutes

Cooking Time: 9 minutes

Servings: 2

Ingredients

- 4 ounces mushroom hats
- 1 teaspoon butter, melted
- 4 quail eggs
- ½ teaspoon ground black pepper
- ¼ teaspoon salt

Directions

- Spread the mushroom hats with the butter inside. Then beat the eggs into mushroom hats
- Sprinkle with salt and ground black pepper. Transfer the mushroom hats on the rack
- Lower the air fryer lid. Cook the meat for 7 minutes at 365 F
- Check the mushroom, if it is not cooked fully then cook them for 2 minutes more
- Serve and enjoy!

Nutrition:

Calories: 190,

Fats: 10g,

Dietary Fiber: 3.1g,

Carbohydrates: 25.5g,

Protein: 3.2g

110. Buttery Corn on the Cob

Preparation Time: 15 minutes

Cooking Time: 15 minutes

Servings: 6

Ingredients:

- 6 large ears of corn, shucked
- 1 cup whole milk
- 3 tablespoons butter, melted
- Salt
- Black pepper

Directions:

1. Fill a large pot halfway with water. Bring to a boil over medium-high heat.

2. Add the corn (the cobs can be cut in half if you want) and milk. Turn heat to medium and then cook the corn for 6 to 10 minutes, depending on how tender you like it, with a few more minutes if you like it more tender.

3. Turn the heat off, but you can keep the corn warm in the pot for up to an hour until you're ready to serve it.

4. Remove corn from the water and drizzle the butter over it. Season with salt and pepper to taste.

5. Technique Tutorial: Here is the easiest way to shuck corn. Cut off the stalk end of each cob right above the first row of kernels with a sharp knife. Place 3 ears of corn on a microwave-safe plate. Microwave for about 60 seconds. Hold the corn by the uncut end in one hand while shaking the ear up and down until the cob slips free, leaving the husk and silk behind. Repeat the other 3 ears of corn.

Nutrition: Calories: 160 Carbs: 36g Fat: 3g Protein: 6g

111.   Simply Roasted Asparagus

Preparation Time: 5 minutes

Cooking Time: 20 minutes

Servings: 6

Ingredients:

- 2 pounds asparagus, trimmed
- 2 tablespoons olive oil
- 1 teaspoon garlic powder
- ½ teaspoon salt
- ¼ teaspoon black pepper

Directions:

1. Preheat the oven to 400°F.
2. In a large bowl, put the asparagus with olive oil and sprinkle with garlic powder, salt, and pepper. Make sure to coat well. Place on a large rimmed baking sheet.
3. Roast it for 15 minutes or until the asparagus is as tender as you like it.
4. Ingredient Tip: Pick bunches of asparagus that have a rich green color and purple highlights with a small amount of white on the bottom. Stalks must be firm, and the tips should not be mushy. To trim the asparagus, just snap off the bottoms as the perfect amount of the stalk will snap right off. It is best not to store asparagus for more than a few days and to cook it as soon as possible.

Nutrition: Calories: 76 Carbs: 12g Fat: 2g Protein: 6g

112.   Honey Glazed Carrots

Preparation Time: 5 minutes

Cooking Time: 25 minutes

Servings: 6

Ingredients:

- 1 pound carrots, peeled
- ½ teaspoon salt
- 2 teaspoons dried parsley
- 2 tablespoons butter, melted
- 2 tablespoons honey

Directions:

1. Preheat oven to 425F, then prepare a rimmed baking sheet with parchment paper.
2. Cut the carrots into 2-inch-thick rounds.
3. In a medium bowl, mix salt, parsley, butter, and honey until evenly coated. Spread the carrots on the baking sheet.
4. Bake carrots 20 to 25 minutes or until tender.
5. Easy Variation: Substitute a 1-pound bag of baby carrots for regular carrots.

Then you can skip the peeling and cutting.

Nutrition: Calories: 80 Carbs: 13g Fat: 2g Protein: 0g

113. Creamy Sour Cream Mashed Potatoes

Preparation Time: 5 minutes

Cooking Time: 25 minutes

Servings: 6

Ingredients:

- 3 pounds potatoes, cubbed in 2 inches
- 3 tablespoons butter, plus more if desired
- ¾ cup milk
- ¾ cup sour cream
- 1 teaspoon salt and black pepper

Directions:

1. Place potatoes with water in a pot on medium-high heat. Bring to a boil and reduce the heat to low. Cover and simmer the potatoes for 15 to 20 minutes or until they are tender. Drain the potatoes in a colander and return them to the pot.

2. Add the butter, milk, sour cream, salt, and pepper to the potatoes. Mash it until smooth. Add a little more milk if necessary.

3. Serve topped with an additional pat of butter, if desired.

4. Technique Tutorial: To mash potatoes, use a masher in an up-and-down motion, and keep mashing until you get the desired consistency. Use a wooden spoon to blend them

together after they have been mashed. If you would like extra-creamy potatoes, you can mash the potatoes, then beat them with a hand beater for about 60 seconds or until they are the smoother texture you desire.

Nutrition: Calories: 110 Carbs: 10g Fat: 3g Protein: 3g

114. Mediterranean Spinach Salad

Preparation Time: 10 minutes

Cooking Time: 0 minutes

Servings: 6

Ingredients:

- 10 to 12 ounces baby spinach
- 1 cup canned chickpeas, rinsed and drained
- ½ cup crumbled feta cheese
- 2 cups grape tomatoes
- ⅓ cup Simple Italian Vinaigrette or your favorite bottled vinaigrette

Directions:

1. In a large bowl, mix the spinach, chickpeas, cheese, and tomatoes.

2. Toss the salad with the dressing right before serving.

3. Prep Tip: Baby spinach is sold in 6-ounce bags and 10-ounce bags. Use either two smaller bags or one larger bag. You can usually find bags of prewashed spinach that is ready to add to your salad.

Nutrition: Calories: 548 Carbs: 57g Fat: 27g Protein: 21g

115. Italian Wedge Salad

Preparation Time: 10 minutes

Cooking Time: 0 minutes

Servings: 4

Ingredients:

- ½ head iceberg lettuce
- 1 cup grape tomatoes, halved
- 6 ounces diced salami
- 6 ounces diced provolone cheese
- ⅓ cup Simple Italian Vinaigrette or your favorite bottled vinaigrette
- Optional: ½ cup sliced black olives

Directions:

1. Cut the lettuce into 4 equal wedges. Place in an individual plates or on a large platter.
2. Top each lettuce wedge with evenly divided amounts of tomatoes, salami, and cheese. Drizzle the dressing on the salads.
3. Top with black olives, if desired.
4. Prep Tip: Buy the salami and provolone cheese from the deli section at your grocery store. You can get it thickly sliced, then just dice it up before tossing it in the salad.

Nutrition: Calories: 200 Carbs: 2g Fat: 10g Protein: 0g

116. Tomato and White Bean Salad

Preparation Time: 10 minutes

Cooking Time: 0 minutes

Servings: 6

Ingredients:

- 1 can white beans
- 1 pint grape tomatoes, halved
- 3 tablespoons chopped fresh basil
- ⅓ Cup crumbled feta cheese
- ¼ cup Simple Italian Vinaigrette or your favorite bottled vinaigrette
- Black pepper

Directions:

1. In a bowl, mix the beans, tomatoes, basil, and cheese.
2. Drizzle the dressing over the salad and mix well.
3. Add pepper to taste.
4. Leftovers: Store leftovers overnight in an airtight container in the refrigerator. This salad is great served on a bed of greens for lunch the next day.

Nutrition: Calories: 220 Carbs: 41g Fat: 1g Protein: 15g

117. Spicy Cucumber Salad

Preparation Time: 10 minutes

Cooking Time: 0 minutes

Servings: 4

Ingredients:

- 2 tablespoons rice vinegar
- 1 teaspoon sea salt
- 1 tablespoon sugar
- 1 tablespoon sesame oil
- 1 large English cucumber, ends trimmed, thinly sliced

- Pinch red pepper flakes

Directions:

1. Mix the rice vinegar, salt, sugar, and sesame oil until the sugar dissolves in a bowl.

2. Add the cucumber slices and red pepper to the bowl. Mix and season with more salt, if desired.

3. Refrigerated before serving.

4. Ingredient Tip: English cucumbers are large, seedless cucumbers found in the produce section of the grocery store. You can substitute 3 smaller pickling (kirby) cucumbers, if you can't find English cucumbers.

Nutrition: Calories: 60 Carbs: 5g Fat: 3g Protein: 4g

118. <u>Strawberry Blue Cheese Arugula Salad</u>

Preparation Time: 10 minutes

Cooking Time: 0 minutes

Servings: 4

Ingredients:

- 3 tablespoons olive oil

- 2 tablespoons balsamic vinegar

- 1 tablespoon honey

- 6 ounces arugula

- 2 cups sliced strawberries

- ⅓ Cup crumbled blue cheese

- Pinch Salt and Black pepper

Directions:

1. In a bowl, mix oil, vinegar, and honey for about 30 seconds or until well blended. Set aside.

2. Put the arugula in a large bowl. Top with the strawberries. Add the dressing and toss well, so all the greens and strawberries are coated. You can use more or less dressing, depending on your taste.

3. Sprinkle the cheese on top.

4. Season with salt and pepper to taste.

5. Simple Swap: For a tangy variation, use feta or goat cheese instead of blue cheese.

Nutrition: Calories: 100 Carbs: 3g Fat: 9g Protein: 3g

119. <u>Cucumber Hummus Wraps</u>

Preparation Time: 10 minutes

Cooking Time: 0 minutes

Servings: 4

Ingredients:

- ½ cup hummus

- 4 thin flatbread wraps or large tortillas

- 1 small cucumber, ends trimmed, thinly sliced

- ⅓ Cup chopped olives

- ¼ cup crumbled feta cheese with Mediterranean herbs

- Optional: roasted red peppers, baby spinach, thinly sliced tomatoes

Directions:

1. Spread hummus on one side of each flatbread or tortilla.

2. Top each with equally divided amounts of cucumbers, olives, and cheese.

3. Add any optional ingredients desired before rolling.

4. Roll each flatbread or tortilla tightly, making sure to tuck in the sides.

5. Leftovers Prep Tip: These wraps are perfect to make for lunch the night before because the flavors will blend together better. Make the wraps, then tightly wrap in foil. Your lunch is now ready for the next day.

Nutrition: Calories: 149 Carbs: 20g Fat: 6g Protein: 5g

120. White Bean Salad

Preparation Time: 3 minutes

Cooking Time: 0 minutes

Servings: 2

Ingredients:

- 1 can white beans, small
- 2 handful lambs lettuce
- 1 tablespoon mustard
- 1 tablespoon agave syrup
- 1 tablespoon balsamic vinegar

What you'll need from the store cupboard

- 1 orange
- 2 tablespoons olive oil
- ½ tablespoon thyme

- 1 pinch salt

Directions:

1. Drain the white beans, then rinse them.

2. Wash the lettuce thoroughly.

3. Peel and slice the orange.

4. Mix all the ingredients in a bowl.

5. All done, your salad is now ready. Serve and enjoy.

Nutrition: Calories 360 Fat 15g Carbs 45g Protein 14g

121. Quick White Bean Salad

Preparation Time: 10 minutes

Cooking Time: 0 minutes

Servings: 4

Ingredients:

- 1 can white beans
- 1 red onion
- 1 bell pepper, red
- 1 handful parsley, fresh
- 1 handful cilantro, fresh

What you'll need from the store cupboard

- 4 tomatoes, sun-dried
- 3 tablespoons olive oil
- 1 tablespoon lemon juice
- Salt to taste
- Pepper to taste

Directions:

1. Drain the beans and rinse them.

2. Dice the onions.

3. Wash the pepper and slice it into small pieces.

4. Slice the sun-dried tomatoes into small strips.

5. Add all the five ingredients with tomatoes into a bowl.

6. Add olive oil, lemon juice, then season with salt and pepper.

7. Serve with whole wheat bread if you desire.

Nutrition: Calories 389 Fat 22g Carbs 40g Protein 12g

122. **Easy Green Bean Salad**

Preparation Time: 10 minutes

Cooking Time: 0 minutes

Servings: 4

Ingredients:

- 1 jar green beans, medium
- 2 tablespoons vinegar
- 1 tablespoons sugar
- 1 handful parsley
- 1 red onion

What you'll need from the store cupboard

- 3 tablespoons olive oil
- ½ tablespoons salt
- ½ tablespoons pepper

Directions:

1. Drain the green beans and save the drained water.

2. Thinly slice the onion, then put it in a large bowl. Add the drained beans to the bowl.

3. Chop parsley and add it along with other ingredients in the bowl.

4. Mix the ingredients, then let rest for two to three hours.

5. Serve and enjoy.

Nutrition: Calories 254 Fat 21g Carbs 15g Protein 2g

123. **Supercharging   Avocado Chickpea Salad**

Preparation Time: 5 minutes

Cooking Time: 0 minutes

Servings: 2

Ingredients:

- 1 can chickpeas
- 2 avocados
- 1 handful cilantro
- ½ red onion
- ½ cup feta cheese

What you'll need from the store cupboard

- 1 lime juice
- Salt to taste
- Pepper to taste

Directions:

1. Drain the chickpeas and rinse them.

2. Dice the avocados and chop the cilantro.

3. Dice the onion, then throw the chickpeas, cilantro, and onion in a large bowl.

4. Add cheese and lime juice to the bowl.

5. Season with salt and pepper to taste, then mix the ingredients. Serve and enjoy.

Nutrition: Calories 708 Fat 46g Carbs 57g Protein 19g

124. Watermelon Salad

Preparation Time: 5 minutes

Cooking Time: 0 minutes

Servings: 3

Ingredients:

- 3 cups cubed melon
- 3 tablespoons rice vinegar
- 1 tablespoon fresh basil, sliced thinly
- 1 tablespoon fresh mint, chopped
- 1 tablespoon fresh cilantro, chopped

What you'll need from the store cupboard

- Sea salt to taste

Directions:

1. Place the watermelon in a colander, then sprinkle salt as you toss the watermelon.
2. Let it rest so that some liquid will drain out.
3. Toss the watermelon with rice vinegar; 1 tablespoon of vinegar per one cup of melon.
4. Add herbs and mix well.
5. Serve and enjoy it when cold.

Nutrition: Calories 48 Fat 0g Carbs 12g Protein 1g

125. 5-Ingredient Vegetable Fried Brown Rice

Preparation Time: 5 minutes

Cooking Time: 15 minutes

Servings: 4

Ingredients:

- 1 cup mixed vegetables (frozen)
- 2 cups brown rice (cooked)
- 2 lightly whisked eggs
- ¼ - ⅓ cup of soy sauce (low-sodium)

What you'll need from store cupboard

- 1 tablespoon coconut oil
- Salt to taste
- Fresh ground pepper to taste

Directions:

1. Heat oil in a frying pan (large) over medium-high heat.
2. Add mixed vegetables, then cook for about 2 minutes while stirring.
3. Add rice and soy sauce. Cook for 5 minutes until heated through.
4. Make a well in the mixture center, then add eggs to the frying pan.
5. Let eggs cook for 1 minute. Use a spoon to break them up into small pieces.
6. Season with additional soy sauce, pepper, and salt to taste.
7. Serve with sriracha and enjoy.

Nutrition: Calories: 279 Fat: 8g Carbs: 45.8g Protein: 10.5g

126. Garlic Roasted Carrots

Preparation Time: 5 minutes

Cooking Time: 40 minutes

Servings: 6

Ingredients:

- 24 baby carrots (tops 2-inches trimmed)
- 2 tablespoons balsamic vinegar
- 5 cloves minced garlic
- 1 tablespoon thyme (dried)
- 2 tablespoons parsley leaves (chopped)

What you'll need from store cupboard

- 2 tablespoons olive oil
- Kosher salt to taste
- Black pepper (freshly ground) to taste

Directions:

1. Preheat your oven to 350 F.
2. Coat a baking sheet with nonstick spray.
3. Place carrots on the baking sheet in a single layer.
4. Add vinegar, olive oil, garlic, and thyme, then season with pepper and salt.
5. Toss gently to combine, then place in the oven.
6. Bake for about 40 minutes until tender.
7. Garnish with parsley and serve immediately. Enjoy!

Nutrition: Calories: 59.5 Fat: 4.6g Carbs: 4.3g Protein: 0.4g

127. Baked Parmesan Mushrooms

Preparation Time: 10 minutes

Cooking Time: 15 minutes

Servings: 4

Ingredients:

- 1½ pound cremini mushrooms, thinly sliced
- ¼ cup lemon juice (freshly squeezed)
- 3 minced garlic cloves
- ¼ cup parmesan (grated)
- 2 tablespoons thyme (dried)

What you'll need from store cupboard

- 3 tablespoons olive oil
- Kosher salt to taste
- Black pepper (freshly ground) to taste

Directions:

1. Preheat your oven to 350 F.
2. Coat a baking sheet with nonstick spray.
3. Place mushrooms on the baking sheet in a single layer.
4. Add olive oil, lemon zest, lemon juice, garlic, parmesan, and thyme, then season with pepper and salt.
5. Combine and place in the oven.
6. Set baking for 15 minutes or until tender and brown. Toss occasionally.
7. Serve immediately and enjoy.

Nutrition: Calories: 163.5 Fat: 12.2g Carbs: 10.3g Protein: 6.9g

128. Buttery Garlic Green Beans

Preparation Time: 10 minutes

Cooking Time: 10 minutes

Servings: 4

Ingredients:

- 1 pound trimmed and halved fresh green beans
- 3 minced garlic cloves
- 2 pinches lemon pepper

What you'll need from store cupboard

- 3 tablespoons butter
- Salt to taste

Directions:

1. Place fresh green beans in a skillet (large) then cover with water. Boil over medium-high heat.
2. Reduce to medium-low heat and simmer the beans for about 5 minutes until beans soften lightly.
3. Drain excess water, then add butter and cook for about 3 minutes while stirring until butter melts.
4. Add garlic, stir and cook for about 4 minutes until garlic is fragrant and tender. Season with salt and lemon pepper.

Nutrition: Calories: 116 Fat: 8.8g Carbs: 8.9g Protein: 2.3g

129. Roasted Butternut Squash Puree

Preparation Time: 15 minutes

Cooking Time: 45 minutes

Servings: 4

Ingredients:

- 1 large seeded and halved butternut squash
- 2 cups chicken stock

What you'll need from store cupboard

- Salt to taste
- Black pepper (ground) to taste

Directions:

1. Preheat your oven to 400 F.
2. Place squash on a baking sheet.
3. Roast squash for 45-60 minutes in the oven until slightly brown and tender. Cool until it can be easily handled.
4. Put squash into a blender and blend until smooth.
5. Add ¼ cup chicken stock at a time while blending until smooth.
6. Season with pepper and salt. Serve and enjoy.

Nutrition: Calories: 159 Fat: 0.6g Carbs: 40.3g Protein: 3.7g

130. Irish Bombay Potatoes

Preparation Time: 5 minutes

Cooking Time: 30 minutes

Servings: 4

Ingredients:

- 35 ounces potato, peeled
- 2 tablespoons curry paste
- 2 tablespoons tomato paste
- ½ cup basil, fresh
- 1 garlic clove

What you'll need from the store cupboard

- 1 tbsp salt
- 4 tablespoons oil
- 2 tablespoons curry powder
- 2 tablespoons white vinegar

Directions:

1. Heat your oven to 390F.
2. Quarter the peeled potatoes then place them in a mixing bowl.
3. Add curry paste, tomato paste, salt, oil, curry powder, then mix until the potatoes ate well coated.
4. Layer the potatoes on your oven tray and bake them for fifteen minutes.
5. Add fresh basil and garlic five minutes before the end of cooking. Mix well.
6. Serve with dips. Enjoy.

Nutrition: Calories 288 Fat 14g Carbs 33g, Protein 7g

131. Healthy Mashed Sweet Potato

Preparation Time: 5 minutes

Cooking Time: 20 minutes

Servings: 2

Ingredients:

- 2 sweet potatoes, peeled and chopped
- 2 garlic cloves
- 1 thumb ginger, fresh
- 1 chili pepper
- 1 handful coriander, fresh

What you'll need from the store cupboard

- 6 tablespoons olive oil
- ½ juiced lime

Directions:

1. Add sweet potatoes to boiling and salted water in a saucepan. Let the sweet potatoes cook for twenty minutes.
2. Meanwhile, add olive oil to a small pan. Add chopped garlic cloves and ginger.
3. Make an incision on the chili pepper, or make four incisions on the chili pepper if you like your food spicier.
4. Let the three fry in oil for some few minutes.
5. When the sweet potatoes are cooked, poke them with a knife to make sure they are fully soft.
6. Add the potatoes to the pan and use a spoon to remove the garlic, ginger, and chili pieces from the oil. The heat should be off.
7. Mash all them together until smooth.
8. Serve with coriander and lime juice. Enjoy.

Nutrition: Calories 503 Fat 42g Carbs 31g Protein 2g

132. Spinach Tomato Quesadilla

Preparation Time: 5 minutes

Cooking Time: 10 minutes

Servings: 2

Ingredients:

- 2 whole-grain tortillas

- ½ cup cheddar cheese, sliced
- 1 cup mozzarella cheese, sliced
- 1 tomato
- 1 ½ cup spinach

What you'll need from the store cupboard

- 1 tablespoon homemade pesto

Directions:

1. Spread a layer of homemade pesto over half tortilla.
2. Add a cheese layer on the tortilla.
3. Slice the tomato and a layer on the cheese.
4. Add a layer of spinach on top, then finally another cheese layer
5. Put half of the tortilla on top.
6. Place the tortilla on a hot pan, cover the pan, and heat for four minutes on each side. The cheese should have melted. Serve and enjoy.

Nutrition: Calories 386 Fat 19g Carbs 26g Protein 23g

133. Lentil Tacos

Preparation Time: 5minutes

Cooking Time: minutes

Servings: 6

Ingredients:

- 1 onion, diced
- 2 garlic cloves, diced
- 1 cup brown lentils, cooked
- 2 tablespoons burrito seasoning
- 2 taco shells

What you'll need from the store cupboard

- 2 tablespoons olive oil
- 4 cups of water
- 6 tablespoons salsa
- 1 ½ cups mixed salad
- ½ cup cherry tomatoes, sliced

Directions:

1. Heat olive oil in the saucepan, then fry the onions until soft.
2. Add diced garlic, then drain the lentils and add them.
3. Add seasoning and water, then stir well. Cook until all water has evaporated.
4. Put the taco shells for three minutes.
5. Layer the lentils at the bottom, followed by cheese if you desire, salsa, mixed salad, and finally, the cherry tomatoes. Serve and enjoy.

Nutrition: Calories 239 Fat 13g Carbs 20g Protein 9g

134. Flawless Feta and Spinach Pancakes

Preparation Time: 10 minutes

Cooking Time: 20 minutes

Servings: 4

Ingredients:

- 17 ounces spinach, frozen
- 1 cup flour
- 2 eggs
- 1cup milk
- 5 ounces feta cheese

What you'll need from the store cupboard

- 2 tablespoons butter
- Salt to taste

Directions:

1. Heat a pot on and put it in medium heat. Add the frozen spinach. Stir frequently to deforest the spinach quickly.

2. Add flour, eggs, and milk in a mixing bowl, then use a hand mixer to mix until there are no lumps.

3. Add more milk until consistency is achieved.

4. Heat a nonstick skillet over medium heat.

5. Melt butter and pour the mixture into the pan — Fry for four minutes on each side.

6. Layer the pancake on a plate, then pour the heated spinach on one half of the pancake.

7. Layer cheese slices on the spinach, then fold the pancake. Serve and enjoy.

Nutrition: Calories 361 Fat 18g Carbs 33g Protein 17g

135. Baked Potato Salad

Preparation Time: 10 minutes

Cooking Time: 30 minutes

Servings: 6-8

Ingredients:

- 6 cups cooked potatoes cut into slices
- 1 cup chopped celery
- ⅔ cup brown sugar

- ⅔ cup vinegar
- 1 ⅓ cup water
- Olive oil for cooking

Directions:

1. Preheat the oven to 350 F.

2. Pour an amount of olive oil into the frying pan and turn the heat to medium. Lightly sauté the celery.

3. Add the sugar, vinegar, and water and bring to a boil. Adjust the heat on low and let simmer for 5 minutes.

4. Fill your oven dish with the cooked potato and pour the vinegar sauce over. Make sure the potatoes are completely covered.

5. Bake the potatoes for about 20 minutes in the oven.

6. This dish works both warm and cold.

Nutrition: Calories 250 Fat 19g Carbs 18g Protein 4g

136. Tropical Fruit Salad

Preparation Time: 10 minutes

Cooking Time: 0 minutes

Servings: 2

Ingredients:

- 1 cup of dragon fruit
- 1 cup ripe mango
- 1 tablespoon lime juice
- 12 Strawberries
- 2 Kiwis

Directions:

1. Peel all of the fruits and then chop them into small, bite-sized pieces. Dump all of the chunks of fruit into a large-sized mixing bowl. Drizzle the lime juice over the fruit and toss the fruit gently to coat all of the pieces with the juice. Serve immediately

Nutrition: Calories 154 Fat 1g Carbs 37g Protein 3g

137. Cilantro Lime Coleslaw

Preparation Time: 10 minutes

Cooking Time: 0 minutes

Servings: 5

Ingredients:

- 2 pieces of avocados
- 1 tablespoon garlic, minced
- 14 ounces coleslaw
- ¼ cilantro, fresh leaves, minced
- 2 tablespoons lime juice
- ½ teaspoon salt
- ¼ cup water

Directions:

1. Except for the slaw mix, put all of the ingredients that are listed into a blender.
2. Blend these ingredients well until they are creamy and smooth.
3. Mix the coleslaw mix in with this dressing and then toss it gently to mix it well.
4. Keep the mixed coleslaw in the refrigerator until you are ready to serve. It needs to chill for at least one hour.

Nutrition: Calories 119 Fat 9g Carbs 3g Protein 3g

138. Pesto Pasta Salad

Preparation Time: 5 minutes

Cooking Time: 10 minutes

Servings: 2

Ingredients: Spinach, one cup

- Fusilli pasta, whole wheat, two cups
- Pesto, low fat, four tablespoons
- Salt, one half teaspoon
- Black pepper, one half teaspoon

Directions:

1. Cook the fusilli, letting it get slightly overcooked so it will not be sticky when it is cold. Before draining the pasta, drop in the spinach and let it wilt for two to three minutes. Drain the water off the pasta and spinach and pour it into a bowl. Add the pesto, pepper, and salt and mix everything together well.

Nutrition: Calories 340 Fat 2g Carbs 66g Protein 10g

139. Veggie Hummus Pinwheels

Preparation Time: 10 minutes

Cooking Time: 0 minutes

Servings: 3

Ingredients:

- 3 whole-grain, spinach, flour, or gluten-free tortillas

- 3 large Swiss chard leaves
- ¾ cup Edamame Hummus or prepared hummus
- ¾ cup shredded carrots

Directions:

1. Lay 1 tortilla flat on a cutting board. Place 1 Swiss chard leaf over the tortilla. Spread ¼ cup of hummus over the Swiss chard. Spread ¼ cup of carrots over the hummus.

2. Starting at one end of the tortilla, roll tightly toward the opposite side. Slice each roll up into 6 pieces. Place in a single-serving storage container. Repeat with the remaining tortillas and filling and seal the lids.

Nutrition: Calories 254 Fat 2g Carbs 39g Protein 10g

140. Caramelized Onion and Beet Salad

Preparation Time: 10 minutes

Cooking Time: 40 minutes

Servings: 4

Ingredients:

- 3 medium golden beets
- 2 cups sliced sweet or Vidalia onions
- 1 teaspoon extra-virgin olive oil or no-beef broth
- Pinch baking soda
- ¼ to ½ teaspoon salt, to taste
- 2 tablespoons unseasoned rice vinegar, white wine vinegar, or balsamic vinegar

Directions:

1. Cut the greens off the beets and scrub the beets. In a large pot, place a steamer basket and fill the pot with 2 inches of water. Add the beets, bring to a boil, then reduce the heat to medium, cover, and steam for about 35 minutes, until you can easily pierce the middle of the beets with a knife.

2. Meanwhile, in a large, dry skillet over medium heat, sauté the onions for 5 minutes, stirring frequently. Add the olive oil and baking soda, and continuing cooking for 5 more minutes, stirring frequently. Stir in the salt to taste before removing it from the heat. Transfer to a large bowl and set aside.

3. When the beets have cooked through, drain and cool until easy to handle. Rub the beets in a paper towel to easily remove the skins. Cut into wedges, and transfer to the bowl with the onions. Drizzle the vinegar over everything and toss well.

4. Divide the beets evenly among 4 wide-mouth jars or storage containers. Let cool before sealing the lids.

Nutrition: Calories 104 Fat 2g Carbs 20g Protein 3g

141. Corn Cobs

Preparation Time: 10 minutes

Cooking Time: 2 minutes

Servings: 4

Ingredients:

- 4 ears corn

- 2 cups water
- Salt and pepper to taste
- 1 tablespoon lemon juice
- 1 tablespoon melted butter

Directions:

1. Add water and arrange the corn ears vertically in the Instant Pot.

2. Keep the larger end of the corn ears dipped in the water or arrange diagonally.

3. Make sure that the lid is closed tightly and select the "Manual" function with high pressure for 2 minutes.

4. After the beep, do a Natural release, then remove the lid carefully?

5. Strain the corn ears and transfer them to a platter.

6. Drizzle some lemon juice along with melted butter on top.

7. Sprinkle salt and pepper, then serve hot.

Nutrition: Calories: 158 Carbohydrate: 29.1g Protein: 5.1g Fat: 4.7g

142. **Potato & Cauliflower Mash**

Preparation Time: 5 minutes

Cooking Time: 25 minutes

Servings: 8

Ingredients:

- 3 cups water
- 4 lbs. potatoes (peeled)
- 16 oz. cauliflower florets
- 1 teaspoon coarse rock salt

- 2 tablespoons full cream
- Additional salt and pepper to taste

Directions:

1. Add water, potatoes, cauliflower, and salt to the Instant Pot.

2. Make sure that the lid is closed tightly and select the "Manual" function for 25 minutes with high pressure.

3. After the beep, do a Natural release in 10 minutes and remove the lid.

4. Drain the water from the pot and leave the potatoes and cauliflower inside.

5. Use a potato masher to mash the cauliflower and potatoes in the pot.

6. Stir in cream, pepper, and additional salt and mix them well.

7. Serve and enjoy.

Nutrition: Calories: 204 Carbohydrate: 38.7g Protein: 6.6g Fat: 2.1g

143. **Green Beans Salad**

Preparation Time: 5 minutes

Cooking Time: 7 minutes

Servings: 4

Ingredients:

- ½ oz. dry porcini mushrooms, soaked
- 1 cup water
- 1 lb. green beans, trimmed
- 1 lb. potatoes, quartered
- ½ teaspoon sea salt, divided
- Ground black pepper to taste

Directions:

1. Add water, potatoes, mushrooms, and salt to the Instant Pot.

2. Place the steamer trivet over the potatoes. Arrange all the green beans in the steamer.

3. Make sure that the lid is closed tightly and select the "Manual" function for 7 minutes with high pressure.

4. After the beep, do a Natural release in 10 minutes and remove the lid.

5. Transfer the greens to a platter. Strain the potatoes and mushrooms.

6. Add the potatoes and mushroom to the green beans.

7. Mix gently, sprinkle some pepper and salt on top, and serve.

Nutrition: Calories: 127 Carbohydrate: 27.7g Protein: 4.9g Fat: 0.3g

144. **Instant Mashed Potato**

Preparation Time: 5 minutes

Cooking Time: 18 minutes

Servings: 4

Ingredients:

- 2 cups water

- 6-8 medium potatoes (peeled)

- 1 teaspoon coarse rock salt

- 2 tablespoons full cream

- Additional salt and pepper to taste

Directions:

1. Put some water, potatoes, and salt in the Instant Pot.

2. Make sure that the lid is closed tightly and select the "Manual" function for 18 minutes with high pressure.

3. After the beep, do a Natural release in 10 minutes and remove the lid.

4. Drain the water from the pot and leave the potatoes inside.

5. To smash the potato in the pot use a masher equipment.

6. Stir in cream, pepper, and additional salt and mix them well.

7. Enjoy

Nutrition: Calories: 394 Carbohydrate: 62.5g Protein: 10.3g Fat: 9.9g

145. **Cheesy Jacket Potato**

Preparation Time: 10 minutes

Cooking Time: 20 minutes

Servings: 5

Ingredients:

- 5 medium potatoes

- 2 cups water

- 1 ½ tablespoons butter

- Salt and Pepper to taste

- ¼ cup cheddar cheese, shredded

- ¼ cup mozzarella cheese, shredded

- 1 teaspoon red pepper flakes

Directions:

1. Prick all the potatoes in the center and create a slit on top.

2. Top the potatoes with cheeses, butter, salt, pepper, and pepper flakes.

THE COMPLETE VEGETARIAN COOKBOOK

3. Add water to the Instant Pot and place a steamer trivet inside.

4. Arrange stuffed potatoes over the trivet with their pricked side up.

5. Secure the lid and cook on the "Manual" function for 20 minutes at high pressure.

6. When the timer goes off, do a 'Natural release' and remove the lid.

7. Transfer the potatoes to the platter and sprinkle with some salt and pepper.

8. Serve and enjoy.

Nutrition: Calories: 205 Carbohydrate: 33.8g Protein: 5.5g Fat: 5.9g

146. **Green Beans with Tomatoes**

Preparation Time: 5 minutes

Cooking Time: 7 minutes

Servings: 8

Ingredients:

- 2 tablespoons olive oil
- 2 garlic cloves, crushed
- 4 cups fresh tomatoes, diced
- 2 lbs. green beans
- Salt to taste

Directions:

1. Add oil and garlic to the Instant Pot and "Sauté" for 1 minute.

2. Stir in tomatoes and sauté for another minute.

3. Set the steamer trivet in the pot and arrange green beans over it.

4. Secure the lid and select the "Manual" function with high pressure for 5 minutes.

5. After it is done, do a Natural release to release the steam.

6. Remove the lid and the trivet along with green beans.

7. Add the beans to the tomatoes in the pot.

8. Sprinkle salt and stir well. Serve hot.

Nutrition: Calories: 82 Carbohydrate: 11.8g Protein: 2.9g Fat: 3.8g

147. **Wine-glazed Mushrooms**

Preparation Time: 5 minutes

Cooking Time: 6 minutes

Servings: 6

Ingredients:

- 2 tablespoons olive oil
- 6 garlic cloves, minced
- 2 lbs. fresh mushrooms, sliced
- 1/3 cup balsamic vinegar
- 1/3 cup white wine
- Salt and black pepper to taste

Directions:

1. Put some oil and garlic in the Instant Pot and Select the "Sauté" function to cook for 1 minute.

2. Now add all the remaining ingredients to the cooker.

3. Switch the cooker to the "Manual" function with high pressure and 5 minutes cooking time.

4. After it is done, do a Quick release, then remove the lid?

5. Sprinkle some salt and black pepper if desired, then serve.

Nutrition: Calories: 91 Carbohydrate: 6.5g Protein: 5g Fat: 5.1g

148.   Steamed Garlic Broccoli

Preparation Time: 5 minutes

Cooking Time: 10 minutes

Servings: 6

Ingredients:

- 6 cups broccoli florets
- 1 cup water
- ½ garlic cloves, minced
- 2 tablespoons peanut oil
- 2 tablespoons Chinese rice wine
- Fine Sea Salt, to taste
- Lemon slices to garnish

Directions:

1. Put some water into the insert of Instant Pot.

2. Place the steamer trivet inside.

3. Arrange the broccoli florets over the trivet.

4. Make sure that the lid is close tightly and select the "Manual" function with low pressure for 5 minutes.

5. After the beep, do a Natural release and remove the lid.

6. Strain the florets and return them back to the pot. Add the remaining ingredients to the broccoli.

7. Select "Sauté" and stir-fry for 5 minutes.

8. Garnish with lemon slices and serve.

Nutrition Calories: 72 Carbohydrate: 6.1g Protein: 2.6g Fat: 4.8g

149.   Lime Potatoes

Preparation Time: 5 minutes

Cooking Time: 10 minutes

Servings: 2

Ingredients:

- ½ tablespoon olive oil
- 2 ½ medium potatoes, scrubbed and cubed
- 1 tablespoon fresh rosemary, chopped
- Freshly ground black pepper to taste
- ½ cup vegetable broth
- 1 tablespoon fresh lemon juice

Directions:

1. Put the oil, potatoes, pepper, and rosemary in the Instant Pot.

2. "Sauté" for 4 minutes with constant stirring.

3. Put all the remaining ingredients into the Instant Pot.

4. Make sure that the lid is closed tightly and select the "Manual" function for 6 minutes with high pressure.

5. Do a quick release after the beep and then remove the lid.

6. Give a gentle stir and serve warm.

Nutrition: Calories: 225 Carbohydrate: 43.3g Protein: 5.1g Fat: 4.1g

150.   Brussels Sprout Salad

Preparation Time: 5 minutes

Cooking Time: 5 minutes

Servings: 8

Ingredients:

- 2 lbs. Brussels sprouts, trimmed and halved
- 1 tablespoon unsalted butter, melted
- 1 cup water
- 2 cups pomegranate seeds
- ½ cup almonds, chopped

Directions:

1. Put some water into the insert of Instant Pot.
2. Place the steamer trivet inside.
3. Arrange the Brussels sprouts over the trivet.
4. Make sure that the lid is close tightly and select the "Manual" function with high pressure for 5 minutes.
5. After the beep, do a Natural release and remove the lid.
6. Transfer the sprouts to a platter and pour melted butter on top.
7. Sprinkle almonds and pomegranate seeds on top and serve.

Nutrition: Calories: 196 Carbohydrate: 35.6g Protein: 5.1g Fat: 4.8g

151.   Instant Sweet Potato

Preparation Time: 5 minutes

Cooking Time: 10 minutes

Servings: 2

Ingredients:

- 1 cup water
- 2 medium sweet potatoes, peeled
- Salt and pepper to taste
- 1 tablespoon olive oil
- 2 tablespoons chopped fresh parsley to garnish
- Pomegranate seeds as needed to garnish

Directions:

1. Put some water into the insert of Instant Pot.
2. Place the steamer trivet inside.
3. Arrange the sweet potatoes over the trivet.
4. Secure the lid and select the "Steam" function for 10 minutes.
5. After the beep, do a Natural release and remove the lid.
6. Remove the potatoes and cut them into cubes.
7. Add oil and potatoes into the Instant Pot and "Sauté" for 5 minutes while stirring.
8. Garnish with parsley and pomegranate seeds.
9. Serve

Nutrition: Calories: 100 Carbohydrate: 23g Protein: 2g Fat: 0g

152. Maple-glazed Brussels sprouts

Preparation Time: 10 minutes

Cooking Time: 4 minutes

Servings: 4

Ingredients:

- 1 lb. Brussels sprouts (trimmed)
- 2 tablespoons freshly squeezed orange juice
- ½ teaspoon grated orange zest
- ½ tablespoon Earth Balance buttery spread
- 1 tablespoon maple syrup
- Salt and black pepper to taste

Directions:

1. Put all the ingredients in the Instant Pot.
2. Make sure that the lid is closed tightly and select the "Manual" function for 4 minutes with high pressure.
3. Do a quick release after the beep and then remove the lid.
4. Stir well and serve immediately.

Nutrition: Calories: 166 Carbohydrate: 14.5g Protein: 3.9g Fat: 11.4g

153. Spaghetti Squash

Preparation Time: 5 minutes

Cooking Time: 20 minutes

Servings: 2

Ingredients:

- 1 (2 lbs.) spaghetti squash

- 1 cup water
- 2 tablespoons fresh cilantro to garnish (optional)

Directions:

1. Slice the squash in half. Remove the seeds from its center.
2. Put some water into the insert of Instant Pot and place the trivet inside.
3. Arrange two halves of the squash over the trivet, with the skin side down.
4. Secure the lid and select "Manual" with high pressure for 20 minutes.
5. After the beep, do a Natural release and remove the lid.
6. Remove the squash and use two forks to shred it from inside.
7. Serve with fresh cilantro.

Nutrition: Calories: 146 Carbohydrate: 32.2g Protein: 3.4g Fat: 2.6g

154. Flavorful Roasted Peppers

Preparation Time: 2 minutes

Cooking Time: 3 hours 20 minutes

Servings: 5

Ingredients:

- 5 medium-sized red bell pepper, cored and halved

Directions:

1. Take a 6-quarts slow cooker, grease it with a non-stick cooking spray and add the peppers.
2. Cover the top, plug in the slow cooker; adjust the cooking time to 3 hours and let it cook on the high heat

setting or until the peppers are softened, stirring halfway through.

3. When done, remove the peppers from the cooker and let them cool off completely.

4. Then remove the pepper peels by tugging them from the edge or with a paring knife.

5. Serve as desired.

Nutrition: Calories: 5 Carbohydrates: 1g Protein: 0g Fats: 0g

155. **Spicy Cajun Boiled Peanuts**

Preparation Time: 5 minutes

Cooking Time: 8 hours

Servings: 15

Ingredients:

- 5 pounds of peanuts, raw and in shells
- 6-ounce of dry crab boil
- 4-ounce of jalapeno peppers, sliced
- 2-ounce of vegetable broth

Directions:

1. Take a 6-quarts slow cooker, place the ingredients in it, and cover it with water.

2. Stir properly and cover the top.

3. Plug in the slow cooker; adjust the cooking time to 8 hours and let it cook on the low heat setting or until the peanuts are soft and floats on top of the cooking liquid.

4. Drain the nuts and serve right away.

Nutrition: Calories: 309 Carbohydrates: 5g Protein: 0g

156. **Savory Squash & Apple Dish**

Preparation Time: 10 minutes

Cooking Time: 4 hours 15 minutes

Servings: 6

Ingredients:

- 8 ounce of dried cranberries
- 4 medium-sized apples, peeled, cored and chopped
- 3 pounds of butternut squash, peeled, seeded and cubed
- Half of a medium-sized white onion, peeled and diced
- 1 tablespoon of ground cinnamon
- 1 1/2 teaspoons of ground nutmeg

Directions:

1. Take a 6-quarts slow cooker, grease it with a non-stick cooking spray, and place the ingredients in it.

2. Stir properly and cover the top.

3. Plug in the slow cooker; adjust the cooking time to 4 hours and let it cook on the low heat setting or until it cooks thoroughly.

4. Serve right away.

Nutrition: Calories: 210 Carbohydrates: 11g Protein: 3g Fats: 5g

CHAPTER 5:

DESSERT RECIPES

157.   Vegan Whipped Cream

Preparation Time: 10 minutes

Cooking Time: 0 minutes

Servings: 2

Ingredients:

- 1 (13- to 14-ounce) can unsweetened, full-fat coconut milk
- 3 teaspoons sugar or any vegan sweetener
- 1 teaspoon pure vanilla extract

Directions:

1. Put the can of full-fat coconut milk overnight in the refrigerator.
2. Place it in a large metal bowl and electric beaters from an electric hand mixer in the freezer for an hour, then prepare the whipped cream.
3. Open a cold can of coconut milk (make sure to not shake it). The coconut cream solids will have hardened on the top. Spoon just the solids into the cold mixing bowl, avoiding the liquid.
4. Use an electric mixer in mixing coconut cream until stiff peaks form.
5. Then add sugar and vanilla, then beat another minute. Taste and add more sweetener if needed.
6. Leftovers: This whipped cream will stay fresh for 3 to 5 days in a sealed container in the refrigerator.

Nutrition: Calories: 41 Fat: 2g Carbohydrate: 6g Protein: 0g

158.   Patty's Three-Minute Fudge

Preparation Time: 10 minutes

Cooking Time: 0 minutes

Servings: 6

Ingredients:

- Vegan butter
- 2 cups dark semisweet vegan chocolate chips
- 1 (14.5-ounce) can vegan sweetened condensed milk
- 1 teaspoon vanilla extract

Directions:

1. Grease an 8-inch square pan with vegan butter and line with parchment paper.
2. In a microwave-safe two-quart bowl, heat the chocolate chips and condensed milk on high for 1 minute. Let rest for a minute, then stir to combine. If needed, heat an additional 30 seconds. Stir until completely melted and the chocolate is smooth. Stir in the vanilla.
3. Pour the fudge into the prepared pan. Make it cool and set for about 1 hour. Then cut into squares.
4. The fudge will keep at room temperature, covered, for 1 to 2 days.

Nutrition: Calories: 89 Fat: 4g Carbohydrate: 12g Protein: 1g

159. Healthy Avocado Chocolate Pudding

Preparation Time: 5 minutes

Cooking Time: 0 minutes

Servings: 4

Ingredients:

- 6 avocados, peeled, pitted, and cut into chunks
- ½ cup pure maple syrup, or more to taste
- ¾ cup unsweetened cocoa powder
- 2 teaspoons vanilla extract
- Fresh mint leaves, optional

Directions:

1. In a food processor, purée the avocados, maple syrup, cocoa powder, and vanilla until smooth.
2. Garnish with mint leaves, if desired.
3. Ingredient Tip: Avoid leftovers and eat it all! The avocado will oxidize and turn brown after just a few hours.

Nutrition: Calories: 578 Fat: 42g Carbohydrate: 58g Protein: 8g

160. Mexican Chocolate Mousse

Preparation Time: 15 minutes

Cooking Time: 0 minutes

Servings: 4

Ingredients:

- 8 ounces bittersweet or semisweet vegan chocolate
- 1¾ cups (about 1 pound) silken tofu
- ½ cup pure maple syrup
- 1 teaspoon vanilla
- 1½ teaspoons ground cinnamon

Directions:

1. Create a double boiler by bringing a medium pot filled halfway with water to a low simmer. Place a heatproof bowl above and make sure it is not touching the water. Add the chocolate to the bowl. Keep the pot over low heat and stir the chocolate until it is melted and silky smooth.
2. In a food processor, add all the ingredients. Blend until smooth.
3. Refrigerate before serving.
4. Substitution Tip: Substitute 1 teaspoon of chili powder for the ground cinnamon or add both for an authentic Mexican chocolate experience.

Nutrition: Calories: 442 Fat: 18g Carbohydrate: 68g Protein: 12g

161. Chocolate Peanut Butter Cups

Preparation Time: 20 minutes

Cooking Time: 0 minutes

Servings: 8

Ingredients:

- 5 ounces vegan semisweet chocolate, divided
- ½ cup smooth peanut butter
- ½ teaspoon vanilla
- ¼ teaspoon salt

Directions:

1. Line a muffin tray with 9 mini or regular paper cupcake liners.

2. Place half the chocolate in a microwave-safe bowl and microwave on high for 25 seconds, then take it out and stir.

3. Place bowl back in the microwave and repeat the process of cooking for 25 seconds, stopping and stirring, until the chocolate has melted.

4. Spoon 1 to 1½ teaspoons of melted chocolate into each cup. Place in the refrigerator for 10 minutes until solid.

5. Stir the peanut butter, vanilla, and salt together in a bowl. Transfer the peanut butter mixture to a resealable plastic bag and seal it tightly. Cut one corner of the plastic bag, then squeeze the bag to pipe 2 to 3 teaspoons of peanut butter in the middle of each cup. Smooth with a small spoon.

6. Melt the remaining chocolate. Spoon 1 to 1½ teaspoons of chocolate into the top of each cup. Smooth with a small spoon.

7. Refrigerate until solid, 30 to 40 minutes. Peel off the liners and enjoy. Remove it from the refrigerator. Let it sit for 15 or a few minutes if you like a softer chocolate.

8. Leftovers: Store leftovers in the refrigerator for up to 2 weeks or in the freezer for up to 1 month.

Nutrition: Calories: 177 Fat: 13g Carbohydrate: 15g Protein: 5g

162. Banana Ice Cream with Chocolate Sauce

Preparation Time: 10 minutes

Cooking Time: 0 minutes

Servings: 4

Ingredients:

- ½ cup raw unsalted cashews
- ¼ cup pure maple syrup
- 1 tablespoon unsweetened cocoa powder
- 1 teaspoon vanilla extract
- ¼ teaspoon salt
- ¼ cup water
- 6 ripe bananas, peeled and frozen

Directions:

1. Place cashews in a bowl and put water. Soak cashews for two hours or overnight. Drain and rinse.

2. In a food processor or blender, place the cashews, maple syrup, cocoa powder, vanilla, and salt. Blend, adding the water a couple of tablespoons at a time until you get a smooth consistency.

3. Transfer to an airtight container, then refrigerate. Bring to room temperature before using.

4. Place frozen bananas in the food processor. Process until you have smooth banana ice cream. Serve topped with chocolate sauce.

5. Ingredient Tip: The best way to freeze a banana is to start with ripe peeled bananas. Slice them into 2-inch chunks and arrange them in a single

layer on a parchment-lined baking sheet. Pop them in the freezer. Once frozen, transfer to freezer-safe bags. Frozen bananas are also a delicious, healthy addition to smoothies. Individually freeze chunks of one banana, and you'll always be ready to create an icy, rich, creamy smoothie.

Nutrition: Calories: 301 Fat: 8g Carbohydrate: 59g Protein: 5g

163. Raspberry Lime Sorbet

Preparation Time: 15 minutes, plus 5 hours or more to chill

Cooking Time: 0 minutes

Servings: 4

Ingredients:

- 3 pints fresh raspberries or 2 (10-ounce) bags frozen
- ½ cup fresh orange juice
- 4 tablespoons pure maple syrup
- 3 tablespoons fresh lime juice
- Dark chocolate curls, optional

Directions:

1. In a glass dish, combine the raspberries, orange juice, maple syrup, and lime juice. Stir well to mix. Cover then put in the freezer until frozen solid, about 5 hours.

2. Get it from the freezer and let it sit for 10 minutes. Crush chunks with a knife or large spoon and transfer the mixture to a food processor. Process this until smooth and creamy for 5 minutes. Serve immediately. The sorbet will freeze solid again, but can

be processed again until creamy just before serving.

3. To serve, place a scoop into an ice cream dish. Garnish with fresh raspberries and dark chocolate curls, if using.

4. Preparation Tip: To make chocolate curls, use a vegetable peeler, and scrape the blade lengthwise across a piece of solid chocolate to create pretty, delicate curls. Refrigerate the curls until ready to use.

Nutrition: Calories: 191 Fat: 2g Carbohydrate: 46g Protein: 3g

164. Baked Apples with Dried Fruit

Preparation Time: 10 minutes

Cooking Time: 1 hour

Servings: 4

Ingredients:

- 4 large apples, cored to make a cavity
- 4 teaspoons raisins or cranberries
- 4 teaspoons pure maple syrup
- ½ teaspoon ground cinnamon
- ½ cup unsweetened apple juice or water

Directions:

1. Preheat the oven to 350°F.

2. Place apples in a baking pan that will hold them upright. Put the dried fruit into the cavities and drizzle with maple syrup. Sprinkle with cinnamon. Pour apple juice or water on the apples.

3. Cover loosely with foil and bake for 50 minutes to 1 hour, or until the apples are tender when pierced with a fork.

4. Serving Suggestion: Serve the apples topped with Vegan Whipped Cream.

Nutrition: Calories: 158 Fat: 1g Carbohydrate: 42g Protein: 1g

165. Hemp Seed Brittle

Preparation Time: 10 minutes

Cooking Time: 10 minutes

Servings: 6

Ingredients: ¼ cup hemp seeds

- 2½ tablespoons brown rice flour
- 3 tablespoons melted coconut oil
- 2½ tablespoons pure maple syrup
- Pinch salt

Direction:

1. Preheat the oven to 350°F. Line a baking sheet with parchment paper.

2. In a bowl, combine all ingredients, then mix well. Spread into an even layer on the baking sheet. Try to quickly else edges will burn.

3. Bake for 10 minutes and make sure the brittle doesn't burn. Turn off the oven and leave it for 30 minutes to cool down.

4. When it's completely cooled, break it into bite-size pieces with a sharp knife or your fingers.

5. Leftovers: Store leftovers in a sealed container at room temperature for 5 days or freeze for up to 1 month.

Nutrition: Calories: 151 Fat: 12g Carbohydrate: 9g Protein: 4g

166. Cardamom Date Bites

Preparation Time: 15 minutes, plus time to soak

Cooking Time: 15 minutes

Servings: 8

Ingredients:

- 1 cup pitted dates
- 3 cups old-fashioned rolled oats
- ¼ cup ground flaxseed
- 1 teaspoon ground cardamom
- 3 ripe bananas, mashed (about 1½ cups)

Directions:

1. Preheat the oven to 350°F. Line a baking sheet with parchment paper.

2. In a small bowl, place the dates and cover with hot water. Let it sit until softened, 10 to 30 minutes, depending on the dates, and then drain. Purée in a food processor or blender. Set the date paste aside.

3. In the food processor, grind the oats and ground flaxseed until they resemble flour.

4. In a large bowl, mix together the cardamom and mashed bananas. Stir in the ground oat-flaxseed mixture.

5. Form into walnut-size balls and flatten a little. Place on the baking sheet and form an indentation in the middle using a ¼ teaspoon measuring spoon. Fill each indentation with about ½ teaspoon of date paste.

6. Bake 15 minutes or until the bites are golden.

Nutrition: Calories: 82 Fat: 2g Carbohydrate: 16g Protein: 2g

167. Sweet Potato Pie Nice Cream

Preparation Time: 5 minutes

Cooking Time: 0 minutes

Servings: 2

Ingredients:

- 2 medium sweet potatoes, cooked (see here)
- ½ cup plant-based milk (here or here)
- 1 tablespoon maple syrup
- 1 teaspoon vanilla extract
- ½ teaspoon ground cinnamon

Directions:

1. Line a baking sheet with parchment paper.
2. Remove the skin from the cooked sweet potatoes and cut the flesh into 1-inch cubes. Place on the baking sheet in an even layer, then place in the freezer overnight, or for a minimum of 4 hours.
3. In a food processor, combine the frozen sweet potato, milk, maple syrup, vanilla, and cinnamon.
4. Process on medium speed for 1 to 2 minutes, or until the mixture has been blended into a smooth soft-serve consistency, and serve.

Nutrition: Calories: 155 Total fat: 1g Carbohydrates: 34g Fiber: 5g Protein: 2g

168. Peanut Butter Nice Cream

Preparation Time: 30 minutes

Cooking Time: 0 minutes

Servings: 2

Ingredients:

- 3 frozen ripe bananas, broken into thirds
- 3 tablespoons plant-based milk (here or here)
- 2 tablespoons defatted peanut powder
- 1 teaspoon vanilla extract

Directions:

1. Combine the bananas, milk, peanut powder, and vanilla in a food processor.
2. Process on medium speed for 30 to 60 seconds, or until the bananas have been blended into a smooth soft-serve consistency, and serve.

Nutrition: Calories: 237 Total fat: 3g Carbohydrates: 45g Fiber: 7g Protein: 10g

169. Chocolate-Peppermint Nice Cream

Preparation Time: 30 minutes

Cooking Time: 0 minutes

Servings: 2

Ingredients:

- 3 frozen ripe bananas, broken into thirds
- 3 tablespoons plant-based milk (here or here)
- 2 tablespoons cocoa powder

- ⅛ Teaspoon peppermint extract

Directions:

1. Combine the bananas, milk, cocoa powder, and peppermint in a food processor.

2. Process on medium speed for 30 to 60 seconds, or until the bananas have been blended into smooth soft-serve consistency, and serve.

Nutrition: Calories: 173 Total fat: 2g Carbohydrates: 43g Fiber: 6g Protein: 3g

170. Strawberry-Watermelon Ice Pops

Preparation Time: 5 minutes

Cooking Time: 0 minutes

Servings: 6

Ingredients:

- 4 cups diced watermelon

- 4 strawberries, tops removed

- 2 tablespoons freshly squeezed lime juice

Directions:

1. Combine the watermelon, strawberries, and lime juice In a blender. Blend for 1 to 2 minutes, or until well combined.

2. Pour into 6 ice-pop molds evenly, then insert ice-pop sticks. Freeze for at least 6 hours before serving.

Nutrition: Calories: 61 Total fat: 0g Carbohydrates: 15g Fiber: 1g Protein: 1g

171. Oat Crunch Apple Crisp

Preparation Time: 10 minutes

Cooking Time: 35 minutes

Servings: 6

Ingredients:

- 3 medium apples, cored and cut into ¼-inch pieces

- ¾ cup apple juice

- 1 teaspoon vanilla extract

- 1 teaspoon ground cinnamon, divided

- 2 cups rolled oats

- ¼ cup maple syrup

Directions:

1. Preheat the oven to 375°F.

2. Combine the apple slices, apple juice, vanilla, and ½ teaspoon of cinnamon in a large bowl. Mix well to thoroughly coat the apple slices.

3. Layer apple slices on the bottom of a round or square baking dish. Take any leftover liquid and pour it over the apple slices.

4. Stir together the oats, maple syrup, and the remaining ½ teaspoon of cinnamon until the oats are completely coated in a large bowl.

5. Sprinkle the oat mixture over the apples, being sure to spread it out evenly so that none of the apple slices are visible.

6. Set 35 minutes to bake or until the oats begin to turn golden brown and serve.

Nutrition: Calories: 213 Total fat: 2g Carbohydrates: 47g Fiber: 6g Protein: 4g

172. Blackberry Ice Cream

Preparation Time: 5 minutes

Cooking Time: 0 minutes

Servings: 1

Ingredients:

- 1 ½ peeled and frozen banana
- 1 cup frozen blackberries
- 1 tbsp. plant-based protein powder
- Fresh mint leaves
- Ice cubes

Directions:

1. In your food processor, blend the frozen berries and banana until it starts to form a single mass.
2. Add the mint leaves and protein powder. Add one or two ice cubes and pulse to help the ingredients blend better.
3. Serve immediately.

Nutrition: Calories: 210 Total fat: 19g Carbohydrates: 13g Protein: 2g

173. Chocolate Pudding

Preparation Time: 5 minutes

Cooking Time: 0 minutes

Servings: 2

Ingredients:

- 1 avocado
- 1 ripe banana
- 4 tbsp. cocoa powder
- 2 tbsps. Dark maple syrup

Directions:

1. Blend the avocado, banana, cocoa powder, and maple syrup in your food processor until everything is thoroughly blended.
2. Chill at least for 30 minutes in the fridge before serving.

Nutrition: Calories: 110 Total fat: 23g Carbohydrates: 2g Protein: 0g

174. Chocolate Brownies

Preparation Time: 5 minutes

Cooking Time: 25 minutes

Servings: 12

Ingredients:

- 2 bananas
- ½ cup cashew butter
- ¼ cup dark maple syrup
- ¼ cup cocoa powder
- 1 ½ tbsp. plant-based, vanilla-flavored protein powder

Directions:

1. Preheat the oven to 350 F.
2. Mash the bananas with a fork in a bowl. Add the cashew butter, maple syrup, cocoa powder, and mix well until a batter forms.
3. Put batter into the dish and bake for 20 - 25 minutes, according to your preferences. Turn around after the first 15 minutes.

4. Let the brownies cool down before cutting them into squares. Enjoy and serve!

Nutrition: Calories: 223 Total fat: 21g Carbohydrates: 15g Protein: 3g

175.   Salted Caramel Coconut Balls

Preparation Time: 15 minutes

Cooking Time: 25 minutes

Servings: 12 balls

Ingredients:

- 1 cup pitted dates
- 1 cup almonds
- ¼ cup coconut flakes
- ¼ tsp. salt

Directions:

1. Blend the dates, almonds, and salt until a sticky dough forms in your food processor.
2. Divide dough into 12. Roll this to make balls. Roll the balls in the coconut flakes, making sure they're completely covered, and serve.

Nutrition: Calories: 33 Total fat: 3g Carbohydrates: 1g Protein: 0g

176.   Baked Pears

Preparation Time: 5 minutes

Cooking Time: 25 minutes

Servings: 2

Ingredients:

- 2 halved pears
- 1 tsp dark syrup

- Cinnamon

Directions:

1. Preheat the oven to 350 F.
2. Scoop the seeds out of your pears and place them in your baking tray. Drizzle with syrup and sprinkle with cinnamon.
3. Bake for 20 - 25 minutes and serve while warm.

Nutrition: Calories: 208 Total fat: 498g Carbohydrates: 3g Protein: 0g

177.   Chocolate Mousse

Preparation Time: 15 minutes

Cooking Time: 0 minutes

Servings: 6

Ingredients:

- 150 g chocolate
- 2 ripe avocados
- 5 oz. coconut cream
- 3 tbsps. dark syrup
- 2 tbsps. cocoa powder

Directions:

1. Melt the chocolate using the Bunsen burner method. Remove the bowl from the heat and let cool slightly.
2. Place your avocados, coconut cream, syrup, and cocoa powder and pulse until everything is blended.
3. Add chocolate and pulse all over again until the mixture is creamy and smooth.

4. Divide mixture into six small bowls and chill in the refrigerator for 30 minutes.

5. Garnish with grated chocolate and serve.

Nutrition: Calories: 49 Total fat: 10g Carbohydrates: 2g Protein: 2g

178. <u>No Bake Apple Pie</u>

Preparation Time: 5 minutes

Cooking Time: 0 minutes

Servings: 2

Ingredients: 2 chopped red apples

- ¼ cup chopped almonds
- ¼ cup sultanas - 2 tsp. lemon juice
- ½ tsp. cinnamon

Directions:

1. In a bowl, mix the almonds, sultanas, lemon juice, and cinnamon. Toss the apples in the mixture, making sure the apples are completely covered.

2. Plate the dessert, top with a dollop of chilled coconut cream, garnish with some chopped almonds and serve.

Nutrition: Calories: 300 Total fat: 13g Carbohydrates: 17g Protein: 2g

179. <u>Cashew-Chocolate Truffles</u>

Preparation Time: 15 minutes

Cooking Time: 0 minutes

Servings: 12 truffles

Ingredients:

- 1 cup raw cashews, soaked in water overnight

- ¾ cup pitted dates
- 2 tablespoons coconut oil
- 1 cup unsweetened shredded coconut, divided
- 1 to 2 tablespoons cocoa powder, to taste

Directions:

1. In a food processor, combine the cashews, dates, coconut oil, ½ cup of shredded coconut, and cocoa powder. Pulse until fully incorporated; it will resemble chunky cookie dough.

2. Spread the remaining ½ cup of shredded coconut on a plate.

3. Form the mixture into tablespoon-size balls and roll on the plate to cover with the shredded coconut. Transfer to a parchment paper-lined plate or baking sheet. Repeat to make 12 truffles. Place the truffles in the refrigerator for 1 hour to set.

4. Transfer the truffles to a storage container or freezer-safe bag and seal.

Nutrition: Calories: 238 Total fat: 18g Carbohydrates: 16g Protein: 3g

180. <u>Crusty Rosemary Bread</u>

Preparation Time: 10 minutes

Cooking Time: 3 hours and 50 minutes

Servings: 8

Ingredients:

- 10-ounce of all-purpose flour, leveled
- 1 teaspoon of nutritional yeast
- 1 1/2 teaspoons of salt

- 2 tablespoons of chopped rosemary, and more for sprinkling
- 2 tablespoons of olive oil, and more for brushing
- 1 cup of water, lukewarm

Directions:

1. Using a large bowl, place the flour and add the remaining ingredients except for water.

2. Stir properly, add 3/4 cup of water and stir again until the moist dough comes together. Add more water if need be.

3. Cover the bowl with a damp towel and let it sit for 30 minutes in a warm place.

4. Then knead the dough for 3 minutes, return it to the bowl, cover it with a damp cloth and let it sit for another 30 minutes in a warm place.

5. Massage the dough again for 3 minutes, return it to the bowl, cover it with a damp cloth and let it sit for another 2 to 3 hours in a warm place or until the dough expands double in size.

6. Transfers the dough to a clean working space covered with flour and mold it into balls.

7. Then take a large parchment sheet, sprinkle it with flour, and place the dough on it.

8. Brush the top of the dough with olive oil, sprinkle it with rosemary leaves, and lower it into a 6-quarts slow cooker.

9. Cover the top and let the dough rest for 1 hour.

10. Then plug in the slow cooker and let it cook at the high heat setting for 2 hours or until an inserted wooden skewer into the loaf comes out clean, while checking the dough at 45 minutes intervals.

11. Transfer the loaf into a preheated broiler and broil it for 5 minutes or until the top are nicely browned and crusty.

12. Let the loaf cool off on the wire rack before slicing to serve.

Nutrition: Calories: 190 Carbohydrates: 19g Protein: 5g Fats: 11g

181. Chewy Olive Parmesan Bread

Preparation Time: 10 minutes

Cooking Time: 4 hours

Servings: 8

Ingredients:

- 3 cups of bread flour, leveled
- 3/4 cup of diced olives
- 1/2 tablespoon of minced garlic
- 1 teaspoon of nutritional yeast
- 1/4 cup of grated vegetarian Parmesan cheese
- 1 1/2 cups of water

Directions:

1. Using a large bowl, place the flour and add the remaining ingredients except for water.

2. Stir properly, add some water and stir again until the moist dough comes together.

3. Cover the bowl with a damp towel and let it sit for 1 1/2 hours in a warm place or until the dough expands double in size.

4. Then take a large parchment sheet, sprinkle it with flour, and place the dough on it.

5. Shape the dough along with the parchment sheet into round balls, cover it with a plastic wrap and let it sit for another 30 minutes.

6. Plug in the slow cooker and let cook at the high heat setting.

7. Drop the dough wrapped in the parchment sheet into the slow cooker and tuck to fit into it properly.

8. Cover the top with a wrapped dish towel or parchment sheets and let it cook for 2 hours at the high heat setting or until an inserted wooden skewer into the loaf comes out clean.

9. Transfer the loaf into a preheated oven at 400 degrees F and bake for 15 to 20 minutes or until the top is nicely browned and crusty.

10. Let the loaf cool off on a wire rack before slicing to serve.

Nutrition: Calories: 110 Carbohydrates: 14g Protein: 2g Fats: 6g

182. <u>Super Tea Spiced Poached Pears</u>

Preparation Time: 10 minutes

Cooking Time: 4 hours and 5 minutes

Servings: 4

Ingredients:

- 4 medium-sized pears, peeled

- 1 tablespoon of grated ginger
- 5 cardamom pods
- 1 cinnamon stick, split in half
- 1/4 cup of maple syrup
- 16 fluid ounce of orange juice

Directions:

1. Cut off the bottom of each pear and centralize it.

2. Using a 4 quarts slow cooker, place the pears in an upright position, and add the remaining ingredients.

3. Cover the top, plug in the slow cooker; adjust the cooking time to 4 hours and let it cook on the high heat setting or until it gets soft.

4. Sprinkle it with the ground cinnamon over each pear, top it with the nuts and serve.

Nutrition: Calories: 98 Carbohydrates: 26g Protein: 1g Fats: 0g

183. <u>Warming Baked Apples</u>

Preparation Time: 10 minutes

Cooking Time: 2 hours and 10 minutes

Servings: 5

Ingredients:

- 4 medium-sized apples
- 1/2 cup of granola
- 4 teaspoon of maple syrup
- 2 tablespoons of melted vegan butter, unsalted

Directions:

1. Cut off the top of the apple and remove the core from each apple using a measuring spoon.

2. Fill the center of each apple with 1/8 cup of granola and place it in a 4-quarts slow cooker.

3. Drizzle with butter and then sprinkle with a teaspoon maple syrup over each apple.

4. Cover the top, plug in the slow cooker; adjust the cooking time to 2 hours and let it cook on the high heat setting or until it gets tender.

5. Serve right away.

Nutrition: Calories: 162 Carbohydrates: 42g Protein: 0.5g Fats: 0.3g

CHAPTER 6:

SNACK RECIPES

184. Lemon and Olive Pasta

Preparation Time: 5 minutes

Cooking Time: 7-8 minutes

Servings: 2

Ingredients:

- 1 Vidalia onion, diced
- 2 garlic cloves, minced
- 1 tablespoon olive oil
- 3½ cups water or unsalted vegetable broth
- 10 ounces bow ties, small shells, or other small pasta (about 3¾ cups)
- Grated zest and juice of 1 lemon
- ¼ cup pitted black olives, chopped
- Salt
- Freshly ground black pepper

Directions:

1. On your electric pressure cooker, select Sauté. Add the onion, garlic, and olive oil. Cook for 7 to 8 minutes, stir until the onion is lightly browned.

2. Add the water and pasta. Cancel Sauté.

3. Close and lock lid, then ensure the pressure valve is sealed, then select High Pressure and set the time for 4 minutes.

4. Once cooked, quickly release the pressure, being careful not to get your fingers or face near the steam release.

5. Once done, carefully unlock, then remove the lid. Stir the pasta and drain any excess water. Stir in the lemon zest and juice and the olives. Taste and add more olive oil and season with salt and pepper.

Nutrition: Calories: 414 Total fat: 7g Protein: 15g Sodium: 436mg Fiber: 9g

185. Cheesy Macaroni

Preparation Time: 10 minutes

Cooking Time: 5 minutes

Servings: 4

Ingredients:

- 1 pound macaroni or other small pasta
- 5½ cups water, divided
- ½ to 1 teaspoon salt, plus more as needed
- 2 yellow potatoes or red potatoes, peeled and cut into chunks
- 2 carrots, cut into chunks (of similar size to the potatoes)
- ½ cup nondairy milk
- ¼ cup nutritional yeast
- 1 tablespoon freshly squeezed lemon juice
- 2 teaspoons onion powder
- 1 teaspoon garlic powder
- Pinch red pepper flakes or cayenne (optional)

Directions:

1. Using an electric pressure cooker pot, combine the macaroni, 4 cups of water, and a pinch of salt.

2. Place trivet in a pot and put potatoes and carrots in a steaming basket on top of the trivet. Close and lock the lid

to ensure the pressure valve is sealed. Select high pressure, then set the time for 5 minutes.

3. Once done, release the pressure carefully not to get your fingers or face near the steam release.

4. Once done, remove the lid and carefully pull out the steaming basket with the potatoes and carrots. Transfer it to a blender, then add the milk, remaining 1½ cups of water, salt, nutritional yeast, lemon juice, red pepper flakes (if using), onion powder, and garlic powder. Purée until smooth. Stir the cheese sauce into the macaroni. Taste and season with more salt or other seasonings, if needed.

Nutrition: Calories: 501 Total fat: 3g Protein: 23g Sodium: 346mg Fiber: 14g

186. <u>Creamy Mushroom Rigatoni</u>

Preparation Time: 10 minutes

Cooking Time: 7-8 minutes

Servings: 4

Ingredients:

- 12 ounce mushrooms, sliced (about 5 cups)
- 2 to 3 teaspoons olive oil
- 3 cups water or unsalted vegetable broth
- ¼ to ½ teaspoon salt, plus more as needed
- 12 ounces rigatoni (about 4½ cups)
- 1 cup unsweetened nondairy milk
- 2 tablespoons nutritional yeast
- 1 tablespoon dried oregano
- 1 teaspoon onion powder
- ½ teaspoon garlic powder
- ¼ teaspoon ground nutmeg (optional)
- Freshly ground black pepper

Directions:

1. On your electric pressure cooker, select Sauté. Add the mushrooms and olive oil and cook for 7 to 8 minutes, stirring occasionally, until the mushrooms are lightly browned. Cancel Sauté.

2. Add the water, salt, and pasta. Close and lock the lid to ensure the pressure valve is sealed, then set the time for 3 minutes in high pressure.

3. Once complete, release pressure naturally for 5 minutes. Quickly release any remaining pressure. Make sure to carefully release.

4. Once done and the pressure is released, remove the lid carefully. Drain off any excess water and stir in the milk, nutritional yeast, oregano, onion powder, garlic powder, and nutmeg (if using). To taste, season it with salt and pepper if needed. You may have to pull apart any noodles that have stuck together.

5. On the pressure cooker, select Sauté or Simmer. Cook for 2 to 3 minutes and stir occasionally until the sauce thickens slightly.

Nutrition: Calories: 506 Total fat: 6g Protein: 23g; Sodium: 200mg Fiber: 12g

187. Southwest Pasta

Preparation Time: 5 minutes

Cooking Time: 5-6 minutes

Servings: 4

Ingredients:

- 1 red onion, diced
- 1 to 2 teaspoons olive oil
- 1 to 2 teaspoons ground chipotle pepper
- 1 (28-ounce) can crushed tomatoes
- 8 ounces rotini, fusilli, or penne
- 1 cup water or unsalted vegetable broth
- 1½ cups fresh or frozen corn
- 1½ cups cooked black beans (from ½ cup dried)
- Salt
- Freshly ground black pepper

Directions:

1. On your electric pressure cooker, select Sauté. Add the red onion and olive oil and cook for 5 to 6 minutes, stirring occasionally, until the onion is lightly browned. Cancel Sauté.

2. Stir in the chipotle pepper, tomatoes, pasta, and water. Make sure lock the lid and the pressure valve is sealed. Select high pressure and set it for 4 minutes.

3. Once cooking is complete, let the pressure release naturally for 4 minutes. Carefully release the remaining pressure. Be careful in using this.

4. Once done and the pressure is released, remove the lid carefully. Stir in the corn and black beans to warm. Taste and season with salt and pepper.

Nutrition: Calories: 366 Total fat: 4 Protein: 17g Sodium: 176mg Fiber: 14g

188. Peanut Noodles

Preparation Time: 10 minutes

Cooking Time: 2 minutes

Servings: 4

Ingredients:

- ½ cup smooth peanut butter
- ¼ cup tamari or soy sauce
- ¼ cup rice vinegar or apple cider vinegar
- 1 to 2 tablespoons toasted sesame oil (optional)
- 1 teaspoon ground ginger (optional)
- Pinch red pepper flakes or cayenne (optional)
- 2½ cups water, plus more as needed
- 8 ounces thick udon noodles or soba noodles
- 4 carrots, cut into matchsticks
- ½ head broccoli, cut into 1-inch pieces

Directions:

1. Stir together the peanut butter, tamari, vinegar, sesame oil (if using), ginger (if using), and red pepper flakes (if using) until smooth and combined in a small bowl.

2. Pour the peanut sauce into your electric pressure cooker's cooking pot. Add the water.

3. Add the noodles to the pot, breaking them into shorter strands if they're too long to lie flat on the bottom and making sure the liquid covers them. Add another ¼ cup of water if needed. Stir the noodles a bit to make sure they don't stick together.

4. Lay the carrots and then the broccoli on top, or put them in a steaming basket on top of a trivet. Close and lock the lid to ensure the pressure valve is sealed. Select Low Pressure and set the time for 2 minutes.

5. When cooking time is complete, make sure to quickly release the pressure, and be careful.

6. Once done and the pressure is released, remove the lid carefully. Toss everything together, breaking up any noodles that may have stuck together, and serve.

Nutrition: Calories: 467 Total fat: 20g Protein: 20g Sodium: 1.5mg Fiber: 5g

189.   Red Curry Noodles

Preparation Time: 5 minutes

Cooking Time: 10 minutes

Servings: 4

Ingredients:

- 2 cups water
- 1 (13.5-ounce) can coconut milk
- ¼ cup red curry paste
- 1 tablespoon freshly squeezed lime juice

- 1 tablespoon tamari or soy sauce
- 1 to 2 teaspoons toasted sesame oil
- 8 ounces thick ramen noodles or wide brown rice noodles

Directions:

1. Using an electric pressure cooker, combine water, coconut milk, curry paste, lime juice, tamari, and sesame oil. Add the noodles, breaking them into shorter strands if they're too long to lie flat on the bottom. Close and lock the lid to ensure the pressure valve is sealed. Select then the high pressure and set it for 1 minute.

2. Once done cooking, remove the lid carefully until pressure is released. Toss everything together, breaking up any noodles that may have stuck together, and serve.

3. Serving tip: Top these yummy noodles with chopped veggies, and pair with greens sautéed in sesame oil.

Nutrition: Calories: 611 Total fat: 36g Protein: 6g Sodium: 473mg Fiber: 2g

190.   Sun-Dried Tomato Pasta

Preparation Time: 10 minutes

Cooking Time: 20 minutes

Servings: 4

Ingredients:

- 1 large Vidalia onion, diced
- 1 teaspoon olive oil, plus more for finishing
- 10 ounces (about 3 cups) penne, rotini, or fusilli

- ¼ cup sun-dried tomatoes, chopped
- 2 cups water or unsalted vegetable broth
- ½ teaspoon salt, plus more as needed
- 2 tablespoons finely chopped fresh basil
- 1 cup cherry tomatoes, halved or quartered
- ½ teaspoon garlic powder (optional)
- Freshly ground black pepper

Directions:

1. On your electric pressure cooker, select Sauté. Add the onion and olive oil and cook for 4 to 5 minutes, stirring occasionally, until the onion is softened.

2. Add the pasta, sun-dried tomatoes, water, and a pinch of salt. Cancel Sauté.

3. Close then lock the lid. Ensure that it is safe, then select high pressure. After, set it for 4 minutes.

4. Once done, release the pressure slowly for 5 minutes. Then release any remaining pressure. Make sure to do some extra precautionary when using a pressure cooker.

5. Once done and the pressure is released, remove the lid carefully. Select Sauté or Simmer. Toss in the basil, cherry tomatoes, garlic powder (if using), and another drizzle of olive oil. Add more salt, if needed, and pepper.

Nutrition: Calories: 343 Total fat: 3g Protein: 14g Sodium: 300mg Fiber: 9g

191. **Tomato Cream Pasta**

Preparation Time: 5 minutes

Cooking Time: 10 minutes

Servings: 4

Ingredients:

- 1 (28-ounce) can crushed tomatoes
- 1 tablespoon dried basil
- ½ teaspoon garlic powder
- 10 ounces penne, rotini, or fusilli (about 3 cups)
- ½ teaspoon salt, plus more as needed
- 1½ cups water or unsalted vegetable broth
- 1 cup unsweetened nondairy milk or creamer
- 2 cups chopped fresh spinach (optional)
- Freshly ground black pepper

Directions:

1. Using a pressure cooker, combine the tomatoes, basil, garlic powder, pasta, salt, and water.

2. Close then lock the lid. Ensure that it is safe, then select high pressure. After, set it for 4 minutes.

3. Once done, release the pressure slowly for 5 minutes. Then release any remaining pressure. Make sure to do some extra precautionary when using a pressure cooker.

4. Once done and the pressure is released, remove the lid carefully. Stir in the milk and spinach (if using).

Taste and season with more salt, if needed, and pepper.

5. On your pressure cooker, select Sauté or Simmer. Cook until sauce thickens for 4 to 5 minutes and the greens wilt.

Nutrition: Calories: 321 Total fat: 3g Protein: 14g Sodium: 365mg Fiber: 9g

192. Penne Arrabbiata

Preparation Time: 10 minutes

Cooking Time: 20 minutes

Servings: 4

Ingredients:

- 1 red onion, diced
- 2 garlic cloves, minced
- 1 teaspoon olive oil
- 1 (28-ounce) can crushed tomatoes
- 1½ cups water
- 10 ounces penne pasta (about 3 cups)
- ½ to 1 teaspoon red pepper flakes
- ½ teaspoon salt, plus more as needed
- Freshly ground black pepper

Directions:

1. On your electric pressure cooker, select Sauté. Add the red onion, garlic, and olive oil. Cook for 4 to 5 minutes and stir occasionally, until the onion is softened.

2. Add the tomatoes, water, pasta, red pepper flakes, and salt. Cancel Sauté.

3. Close then lock the lid. Ensure that it is safe, then select high pressure. After, set it for 4 minutes.

4. Once done, release the pressure slowly for 5 minutes. Then release any remaining pressure. Make sure to do some extra precautionary when using a pressure cooker.

5. Once done and the pressure is released, remove the lid carefully. Add salt and black pepper if needed.

Nutrition: Calories: 327 Total fat: 3g Protein: 14g Sodium: 317mg Fiber: 9g

193. Hummus Noodle Casserole

Preparation Time: 5 minutes

Cooking Time: 15 minutes

Servings: 4

Ingredients:

- 1 cup hummus
- 3¼ to 3½ cups water and/or unsalted vegetable broth
- 10 ounces penne, bow tie, or small shell pasta (about 3 cups)
- 3 or 4 celery stalks, chopped
- ½ teaspoon sweet paprika
- ½ teaspoon dried thyme
- 1 cup peas
- ¼ to ½ cup fresh parsley, finely chopped
- Salt
- Freshly ground black pepper

Directions:

1. Using a pressure cooker, stir together the hummus and water until mostly combined. Add the pasta, celery, paprika, and thyme. If you like your

peas fully cooked, add them here, as well as the parsley if you want it to merge into the sauce.

2. Close then lock the lid. Ensure that it is safe, then select high pressure. After, set it for 4 minutes.

3. Once done, release the pressure slowly for 5 minutes. Then release any remaining pressure. Make sure to do some extra precautionary when using a pressure cooker.

4. Once done and the pressure is released, remove the lid carefully. Stir in the peas and parsley. Season with salt and pepper if desired.

Nutrition: Calories: 434 Total fat: 10g Protein: 16g Sodium: 30mg Fiber: 11g Fat: 7g

194.   Cinnamon Chickpeas

Preparation Time: 8 minutes

Cooking Time: 42 minutes

Servings: 4 to 6

Ingredients:

- 1 cup dried chickpeas
- 2 cups water
- 2 teaspoons ground cinnamon, plus more as needed
- ½ teaspoon ground nutmeg (optional)
- 1 tablespoon coconut oil
- 2 to 4 tablespoons unrefined sugar or brown sugar, plus more as needed

Directions:

1. Soak chickpeas overnight and drain. Rinse the chickpeas, then put them in your electric pressure cooker's cooking pot.

2. Add the water, cinnamon, and nutmeg (if using). Then lock the lid. Ensure that it is safe, then select high pressure. After, set it for 30 minutes.

3. Once done, release the pressure slowly for 15 minutes. Then release any remaining pressure. Make sure to do some extra precautionary when using a pressure cooker.

4. Once pressure is released, carefully remove the lid. Drain any excess water from the chickpeas and add them back to the pot.

5. Stir in the coconut oil and sugar. Taste and add more cinnamon, if desired. Select Sauté and cook for about 5 minutes, stirring the chickpeas occasionally, until there's no liquid left and the sugar has melted onto the chickpeas. Transfer into a bowl, then toss it with additional sugar if you want to add a crunchy texture.

Nutrition: Calories: 253 Total fat: 7g Protein: 11g Sodium: 9mg Fiber: 10g

195.   Black-Eyed Peas and Collard Greens

Preparation Time: 5 minutes

Cooking Time: 50 minutes

Servings: 4 to 6

Ingredients:

- 1 yellow onion, diced
- 1 tablespoon olive oil
- 1 cup dried black-eyed peas

- 2 cups water or unsalted vegetable broth
- ¼ cup chopped sun-dried tomatoes
- ¼ cup tomato paste or natural ketchup
- 1 teaspoon smoked paprika
- Pinch red pepper flakes (optional)
- 4 large collard green leaves
- Salt
- Freshly ground black pepper

Directions:

1. On your electric pressure cooker, select Sauté. Add the onion and olive oil and cook for 3 to 4 minutes, stirring occasionally, until the onion is softened. Add the black-eyed peas, water, tomatoes, tomato paste, paprika, and red pepper flakes (if using) and stir to combine. Cancel Sauté.

2. Close then lock the lid. Ensure that it is safe, then select high pressure. After, set it for 30 minutes.

3. Once done, release the pressure slowly for 15 minutes. Then release any remaining pressure. Make sure to do some extra precautionary when using a pressure cooker.

4. Trim off the thick parts of the collard green stems, then slice the leaves lengthwise in half or quarters. Roll them up together, then finely slice them into ribbons. Sprinkle the sliced collard greens with a pinch of salt and massage it into them with your hands to soften.

5. Once pressure is released, carefully unlock and remove the lid. Add the collard greens and ½ teaspoon of salt to the pot, stirring to combine and letting the greens wilt in the heat. Taste and season with salt and pepper. If you want your greens cooked more, select Sauté again for another few minutes.

Nutrition: Calories: 267 Total fat: 5g Protein: 15g Sodium: 332mg Fiber: 13g

196. Lentil Bolognese Sauce

Preparation Time: 10 minutes

Cooking Time: 40 minutes

Servings: 3

Ingredients:

- 12 ounces mushrooms, sliced (about 4½ cups)
- 1 onion, diced
- 1 tablespoon olive oil or vegan margarine
- ½ cup dry white wine or red wine
- 2 cups dried green lentils
- 1 (28-ounce) can crushed tomatoes
- 2 cups water or unsalted vegetable broth
- ¼ to ½ teaspoon salt
- Freshly ground black pepper

Directions:

1. On your electric pressure cooker, select Sauté. Add the mushrooms, onion, and olive oil and toss to combine. Cover the pot but do not

lock the lid, and cook for 7 to 8 minutes, until the onion and mushrooms are slightly browned. Add wine, then cook again for 1 to 2 minutes until wine is evaporated.

2. Stir in the lentils, tomatoes, and water. Cancel Sauté.

3. Close then lock the lid. Ensure that it is safe, then select high pressure. After, set it for 10 minutes.

4. Once done, release the pressure slowly for 20 minutes. Then release any remaining pressure. Make sure to do some extra precautionary when using a pressure cooker.

5. Once released and pressure is out, carefully remove the lid. Use salt and pepper to taste.

Nutrition: Calories: 303 Total fat: 4g Protein: 19g Sodium: 114mg Fiber: 21g

197.   <u>Feijoada</u>

Preparation Time: 10 minutes

Cooking Time: 1 hour and 5 minutes

Servings: 6 to 8

Ingredients:

- 1 large onion, diced
- 3 or 4 garlic cloves, minced
- 1 tablespoon olive oil
- 2 cups dried black beans
- 4 cups water and/or unsalted vegetable broth
- 1 tablespoon ground cumin
- 1 tablespoon smoked paprika
- 1 tablespoon dried oregano
- Salt
- ¼ cup fresh cilantro, chopped

Directions:

1. On your electric pressure cooker, select Sauté. Add the onion, garlic, and olive oil. Cook for 5 minutes and stir until the onion is softened. Add the black beans, water, cumin, paprika, and oregano, stirring to combine. Cancel Sauté.

2. Close then lock the lid. Ensure that it is safe, then select high pressure. After, set it for 30 minutes.

3. Once done, release the pressure slowly for 30 minutes. Then release any remaining pressure. Make sure to do some extra precautionary when using a pressure cooker.

4. Once pressure is released, carefully remove the lid. Taste and season with ½ to 1 teaspoon of salt. If your beans are not quite soft enough, or if you have too much liquid, select Sauté or Simmer and cook, uncovered, for 10 to 15 minutes more. Stir in the cilantro just before serving.

5. Serve with rice, sautéed collard greens or kale, and orange wedges. For an authentic cultural experience, toast ½ cup cassava flour in 2 to 3 tablespoons coconut oil in a small skillet, then put it in medium heat for 3 to 5 minutes until browned; sprinkle over the finished dish.

Nutrition: Calories: 268 Total fat: 4g Protein: 16g Sodium: 199mg Fiber: 16g

198. Teriyaki Tempeh and Broccoli

Preparation Time: 10 minutes

Cooking Time: 10 minutes

Servings: 2

Ingredients:

- ¼ cup tamari or soy sauce
- ¼ cup water
- 1 tablespoon olive oil
- 1 tablespoon pure maple syrup or unrefined sugar
- 1 teaspoon cornstarch or arrowroot powder
- ½ teaspoon ground ginger
- Fresh ginger
- 1 (8- or 9-ounce) tempeh, cubed
- ½ head broccoli, cut into pieces

Directions:

1. Mix the tamari, water, olive oil, maple syrup, cornstarch, and ginger in a pressure cooker. Add the tempeh. Close and lock the lid, then ensure the pressure valve is sealed. Select high pressure and set for 5 minutes.

2. When cooking is complete, quick release the pressure, being careful not to get your fingers or face near the steam release.

3. Once pressure is released, carefully unlock the lid and mix.

4. Serving tip: For a complete meal, serve this dish with cooked quinoa or Cilantro-Lime Brown and Wild Rice, sprinkled with toasted sesame seeds or cashews. Try garnishing the dish with sliced scallions.

Nutrition: Calories: 336 Total fat: 18g Protein: 25g Sodium: 2g Fiber: 3g

199. Peach Crisp

Preparation Time: 15 minutes

Cooking Time: 2 hours

Servings: 5

Ingredients:

- 3 large peaches, peeled, pitted, and sliced
- ⅓ Cup all-purpose flour
- ⅓ Cup quick-cooking oats
- ⅓ Cup brown sugar
- ½ teaspoon ground cinnamon
- ⅛ Teaspoon ground nutmeg
- 4 tablespoons (½ stick) unsalted butter
- Vanilla ice cream, for serving

Directions:

1. Put the peaches in the slow cooker.

2. Mix the flour, oats, brown sugar, cinnamon, and nutmeg in a bowl. Using the pastry blender, make the butter into the flour mixture until it is crumbly. Sprinkle the mixture over the peaches.

3. Double layer paper towels on top of the slow cooker and secure with the lid. Cook on high for 2 hours.

4. Serve with your favorite vanilla ice cream.

Nutrition: Calories: 207 Total Fat: 10g Cholesterol: 24mg Carbohydrates: 28g Fiber: 2g Protein: 3g

200. Banana Bread

Preparation Time: 15 minutes

Cooking Time: 2 hours and 30 minutes

Servings: 8

Ingredients:

- ⅓ Cup milk
- 3 tablespoons canola oil
- 1 large egg, lightly beaten
- 3 medium ripe bananas, mashed
- 2½ cups all-purpose flour
- ½ cup granulated sugar
- ½ cup brown sugar
- 3½ teaspoons baking powder
- 1 teaspoon salt

Directions:

1. Whisk milk, oil, egg, and mashed bananas together in a bowl. Add the flour, granulated sugar, brown sugar, baking powder, and salt. Mix it until no flour streaks remain.

2. Grease a loaf pan that will fit inside your slow cooker insert. Pour the butter into the loaf pan.

3. Put the trivet in a slow cooker. Place the loaf pan on the trivet. Double layer paper towels on top of the slow cooker and secure with the lid. Cook on high for 2½ hours.

4. Take the loaf pan from the slow cooker and let it sit for 15 minutes. Slice and serve warm.

Nutrition: Calories: 333 Total Fat: 7g Cholesterol: 24mg Carbohydrates: 66g Fiber: 2g Protein: 6g

201. Mexican Beans and Rice

Preparation Time: 5 minutes

Cooking Time: 3 hours

Servings: 4

Ingredients:

- 1 (15-ounce) can black beans
- ¾ cup long-grain brown rice
- 1½ cups water
- ¾ cup salsa
- 1 bay leaf
- 1 teaspoon ground cumin
- ½ teaspoon garlic powder
- ½ teaspoon salt
- 1 to 2 tablespoons fresh lime juice
- Sour cream, for topping (optional)

Directions:

1. Combine the beans, rice, water, salsa, bay leaf, cumin, garlic powder, and salt in the slow cooker.

2. Cook on low for 3 hours.

3. Discard the bay leaf. Add the lime juice and additional salsa, if desired.

4. Serve it a dollop of sour cream.

Nutrition: Calories: 262 Total Fat: 2g Cholesterol: 0mg Sodium: 587mg Carbohydrates: 52g Fiber: 10g Protein: 11g

202. Spaghetti Squash with Feta

Preparation Time: 5 minutes

Cooking Time: 6 hours

Servings: 2

Ingredients:

- 1 small (1- to 2-pound) spaghetti squash
- 1 cup water
- ¼ cup heavy cream
- 3 garlic cloves, minced
- 3 tablespoons unsalted butter
- ½ cup feta cheese
- Salt
- Freshly ground black pepper
- 2 tablespoons chopped fresh parsley, for garnish

Directions:

1. Cut 6 to 8 slits all over the spaghetti squash. Place the squash in the slow cooker. Add the water.
2. Cook on low for 6 hours.
3. Transfer squash to the cutting board and allow it to cool slightly. Once you can handle it, slice the squash lengthwise and remove the seeds. Scrape the flesh to create long strands resembling spaghetti using a fork.
4. Return the squash strands to the slow cooker and turn to low. Add the cream, garlic, and butter and stir gently to combine. Add the feta. Season with salt and pepper. Garnish with chopped parsley and serve.

Nutrition: Calories: 453 Total Fat: 34g Cholesterol: 100mg; Sodium: 705mg Carbohydrates: 35g Fiber: 0g Protein: 9g

203. Zucchini Noodles with Marinara Sauce

Preparation Time: 15 minutes

Cooking Time: 8 hours

Servings: 6

Ingredients:

- 2 (28-ounce) cans crushed tomatoes
- 1 can diced tomatoes
- Green peppers
- Onion
- 1 (6-ounce) can tomato paste
- 1 bay leaf
- 2 teaspoons dried basil
- 1 teaspoon garlic powder
- ½ teaspoon dried oregano
- 1 teaspoon brown sugar
- 2 tablespoons olive oil
- Salt
- Freshly ground black pepper
- 4 medium zucchini, trimmed

Directions:

1. Combine the crushed tomatoes, diced tomatoes with their juice, tomato paste, bay leaf, basil, garlic powder, oregano, and brown sugar in the slow cooker. Stir to combine.
2. Cook on low for 8 hours.

3. Discard the bay leaf. Stir in the olive oil. Season with salt and pepper.

4. Using a spiralizer, make zucchini noodles. Place zucchini noodles in the microwave-safe dish. Set it on high for 3 minutes. Pile the zucchini on individual serving plates and top with marinara sauce.

Nutrition: Calories: 156 Total Fat: 5g Cholesterol: 0mg Sodium: 422mg Carbohydrates: 24g Fiber: 8g Protein: 7g

204. Coconut Curry with Vegetables

Preparation Time: 5 minutes

Cooking Time: 4 hours

Servings: 4

Ingredients:

- 1 (13.5-ounce) can coconut milk, stirred
- 2 tablespoons red curry paste
- 2 tablespoons instant tapioca
- 1 (1-pound) package frozen stir-fry vegetables
- 1 (15-ounce) can chickpeas, rinsed and drained
- Salt
- Freshly ground black pepper

Directions:

1. Combine the coconut milk, curry paste, and tapioca in the slow cooker. Stir until the curry paste is thoroughly blended into the milk. Stir in the vegetables and chickpeas.

2. Cook on low for 4 hours.

3. Season with salt and pepper and serve.

Nutrition: Calories: 483 Total Fat: 28g Saturated Fat: 23g Sodium: 780mg Carbohydrates: 50g Fiber: 11g Protein: 10g

205. Baked Potatoes with Avocado Pico de Gallo

Preparation Time: 5 minutes

Cooking Time: 8 hours

Servings: 6

Ingredients:

- 6 russet potatoes
- ⅓ Cup red onion
- 1 ripe avocado, finely chopped
- ⅓ Cup fresh cilantro
- 4 Roma tomatoes, finely chopped
- 2 tablespoons olive oil
- Salt
- Black pepper

Directions:

1. Rinse the potatoes thoroughly, then dry with paper towels.

2. Poke the russet potatoes using a fork in several places. Rub it with olive oil. Wrap each potato tightly in aluminum foil. Put the potatoes in the slow cooker.

3. Cover the slow cooker, then cook for 8 hours on low, or until the potatoes are tender. Remove potatoes from the slow cooker. Cover the potatoes in a bowl using a clean towel to keep warm.

4. Now, prepare the pico de gallo. Gently mix and stir the onion, tomatoes, cilantro, and avocado in a bowl. Season with salt and pepper.

5. Unwrap each potato and halve lengthwise. Fluff the potato flesh with a fork. Top each potato with a generous portion of pico de gallo and serve.

Nutrition: Calories: 410 Total Fat: 12g Sodium: 50mg Carbohydrates: 72g Fiber: 8g Protein: 9g

206. Flourless Dark Chocolate Cake

Preparation Time: 10 minutes

Cooking Time: 45 minutes

Servings: 6

Ingredients:

- ½ cup of water
- ¾ cup coconut sugar or granulated sugar
- ⅛ Teaspoon of sea salt
- 1¼ pounds bittersweet chocolate (containing at least 60% cacao), roughly chopped
- 1 cup salted butter, cut into 1-inch cubes, plus more for greasing pan
- 7 eggs
- 2 teaspoons pure vanilla extract

Directions:

1. Preheat the oven to 300°F. Grease the springform pan for a 9-inch round and set the pan on a piece of foil. Fold the foil up outside of the pan, forming a waterproof layer. Set aside.

2. Combine the water, sugar, and salt over medium-high heat, stirring in a small saucepan, until the sugar is completely dissolved. Take off the pan from the heat and set it aside.

3. Place the chocolate in a large bowl over a medium saucepan of simmering water and stir until the chocolate has melted.

4. Get the chocolate from the heat. Beat in the butter one at a time using a hand mixer on medium speed until blended.

5. Beat in the sugar mixture and the eggs (one at a time) at medium speed. Add the vanilla and beat until smooth.

6. Prepared springform pan, then place the butter and place the pan into a larger pan. In a larger pan, bring the water to boil until it reaches one inch up the sides of the springform pan.

7. Bake until the edges are firm, about 45 minutes. Take the cake out of the oven and let cool on a rack.

8. Chill the cake in the refrigerator overnight. Remove from the springform pan when ready to serve.

9. Flavor Boost Chocolate and coffee are a popular pairing because the bitterness and sweetness create incredible richness. Stir one tablespoon of espresso powder into the water in step 2 along with the sugar and salt.

10. Then follow the remaining steps as written.

Nutrition: Calories: 416 Fat: 30g Protein: 6g Cholesterol: 138mg Sodium: 192mg Carbohydrates: 40g Fiber: 3g

207. Creamy Peach Ice Pops

Preparation Time: 10 minutes

Cooking Time: 0 minutes

Servings: 8

Ingredients:

- 1 (14-ounce) can light coconut milk
- 2 peaches, peeled, pitted, and roughly chopped
- ¼ cup honey
- Pinch cinnamon

Directions:

1. In a blender, blend the coconut milk, peaches, honey, and cinnamon until smooth.
2. Pour the mixture into ice pop molds and freeze for about 5 hours.
3. Can stored for a week in the freezer using plastic wrap over the open tops of the molds.
4. Substitution Tip: You can create a staggering variety of wonderful flavors by swapping out the peaches for other ingredients—you'll need about 3 cups total. Try peeled plums, watermelon, cantaloupe, berries, sweet potato, mango, pineapple, and papaya in any combination or alone. Add an amount of honey, depending on the sweetness of the base ingredient.

Nutrition: Calories: 79 Total Fat: 3g Protein: 0g Cholesterol: 0mg Sodium: 4mg Carbohydrates: 13g Fiber: 1g

208. Melon-Lime Sorbet

Preparation Time: 15 minutes

Cooking Time: 0 minutes

Servings: 8

Ingredients:

- 1 small honeydew melon, cut into 1-inch chunks
- 1 small cantaloupe, cut into 1-inch chunks
- 2 tablespoons honey
- 2 tablespoons freshly squeezed lime juice
- Pinch cinnamon
- Water as needed

Directions:

1. Spread the honeydew and cantaloupe out on a baking sheet lined with parchment paper, then place in the freezer for up to 4 to 6 hours or until frozen.
2. In a food processor, add the frozen melon chunks and the honey, lime juice, and cinnamon.
3. Pulse and wait until smooth, add water (a tablespoon at a time) if needed to purée the melon.
4. Transfer the mixture to a container that is resalable and place in the freezer until set, about 30 minutes.
5. Substitution Tip: Almost any fruit will work in this recipe. You can try

watermelon, peaches, plums, mangos, or berries. Some fruit has more water in it than others, so if you're using produce that's less juicy, add extra water or apple juice to create a smooth purée.

Nutrition: Calories: 97 Total Fat: 0g Protein: 2g Cholesterol: 0mg Sodium: 39mg Carbohydrates: 25g Fiber: 2g

209.   Mandarin Ambrosia

Preparation Time: 5 minutes

Cooking Time: 0 minutes

Servings: 6

Ingredients:

- ½ cup coconut cream, chilled in the refrigerator overnight
- 3 cups vegan mini marshmallows
- 1 cup shredded unsweetened coconut
- 3 small tangerines, peeled and segmented
- ½ cup sour cream

Directions:

1. In a large bowl, beat the cold coconut cream until it forms stiff peaks.
2. Stir in the marshmallows, coconut, tangerine segments, and sour cream until well mixed.
3. Place it in the refrigerator for 3 hours before serving.

Nutrition: Calories: 285 Total Fat: 22g Saturated Fat: 19g Protein: 4g Cholesterol: 6mg Sodium: 13mg Carbohydrates: 27g Fiber: 3g

210.   Coconut-Quinoa Pudding

Preparation Time: 5 minutes

Cooking Time: 20 minutes

Servings: 6

Ingredients:

- 2 cups almond milk
- 1½ cups quinoa
- 1 cup light coconut milk
- ½ cup maple syrup
- Pinch salt
- 1 teaspoon pure vanilla extract

Directions:

1. Heat the almond milk, quinoa, coconut milk, maple syrup, salt, and vanilla over medium-high heat in a large saucepan.
2. Bring the quinoa mixture to a boil and then reduce the heat to low.
3. Simmer until the quinoa is tender, stirring frequently, about 20 minutes.
4. Remove the pudding from the heat.
5. Serve warm.
6. Flavor Boost: If you are a chocolate enthusiast, stir 1 tablespoon of good-quality unsweetened cocoa powder into the almond milk and coconut milk before you combine the liquids with the other ingredients in step 1. This way you can remove any lumps in the cocoa powder before you add the quinoa.

7. Increase the maple syrup to ¾ cup to offset the bitterness of the powder.

Nutrition: Calories: 249 Total Fat: 6g Protein: 6g Cholesterol: 0mg Sodium: 161mg Carbohydrates: 42g Fiber: 3g

211. Stuffed Pears with Hazelnuts

Preparation Time: 5 minutes

Cooking Time: 20 minutes

Servings: 4

Ingredients:

- 1 tablespoon butter
- 2 ripe pears, cored and hollowed out with a spoon
- ½ cup water
- 8 tablespoons goat cheese
- 2 tablespoons honey
- ¼ cup roughly chopped hazelnuts

Directions:

1. Preheat the oven to 350°f.
2. Melt the butter using a skillet on a medium heat.
3. Place the pears in the skillet, skin-side up, and lightly brown them, about 2 minutes.
4. Place the pears in an 8-by-8-inch square baking dish, hollow-side up, and pour water into the baking dish, make sure not to get any in the hollow part of the pears.
5. Roast the pears until softened, about 10 minutes. Remove the pears from the oven.

6. Using a small bowl, mix goat cheese, honey, and hazelnuts.
7. Divide the goat cheese mixture evenly between the pear halves and put them back in the oven for 5 minutes. Serve warm.

Nutrition: Calories: 185 Total Fat: 9g Protein: 4g Cholesterol: 14mg Sodium: 75mg Carbohydrates: 26g Fiber: 4g

212. Buttermilk Panna Cotta with Mango

Preparation Time: 10 minutes

Cooking Time: 2 minutes

Servings: 4

Ingredients:

- ½ cup full-fat coconut milk
- 1½ teaspoons agar-agar
- 1½ cups buttermilk
- ¼ cup honey
- 2 cups roughly chopped fresh mango

Directions:

1. Pour coconut milk into a saucepan, then sprinkle the agar-agar over it and let the coconut milk stand for 5 minutes.
2. Put the saucepan over medium-low heat until the agar-agar is dissolved, about 2 minutes.
3. Add the buttermilk and honey and stir to combine.
4. Pour the panna cotta mixture into 4 (6-ounce) ramekins. Wrap it in plastic wrap, then refrigerate them for about 3 hours, or until set.

5. Loosen the panna cotta by running a knife around the inside edges of the ramekins. Invert them onto serving plates.

6. Top with mango and serve.

7. Flavor Boost Vanilla beans add intense flavor and a pretty speckled appearance to this creamy dessert. Cut the vanilla bean in lengthwise and use a paring knife to scrape the seeds from one half into the buttermilk and honey in step 3. Wrap the other vanilla bean half in plastic and store in the fridge to use in smoothies or another dessert.

Nutrition: Calories: 226 Total Fat: 8g Protein: 6g Cholesterol: 4mg Sodium: 106mg Carbohydrates: 36g Fiber: 2g

213. Sweet Potato–Cinnamon Parfaits

Preparation Time: 15 minutes

Cooking Time: 15 minutes

Servings: 4

Ingredients:

- 2 sweet potatoes, cut into ½-inch chunks
- 1 cup coconut cream, chilled in the refrigerator overnight
- ¼ cup maple syrup
- ¼ teaspoon ground cinnamon
- Pinch sea salt
- ½ cup roughly chopped hazelnuts

Directions:

1. Get a large saucepan, then put the sweet potatoes. Fill the pan with water until the sweet potatoes are covered by about an inch. Boil over high heat and then reduce the heat and simmer until sweet potatoes are tender, about 15 minutes. Drain the water and mash sweet potatoes until smooth using a potato masher.

2. Transfer the sweet potatoes to a resealable container, and set it in the refrigerator until completely cooled, about 2 hours.

3. Whip the cold coconut cream until stiff peaks form using a large bowl.

4. Mix the sweet potatoes, maple syrup, cinnamon, and salt, then stir together in a bowl until smooth.

5. Fold half the whipped coconut cream into the sweet potato mixture, keeping as much volume as possible.

6. Chill the sweet potato mixture in the refrigerator for 1 hour.

7. Spoon the sweet potato mixture into 4 bowls and divide the remaining whipped coconut cream between the bowls.

8. Top with hazelnuts before serving.

9. Flavor Boost Hazelnuts have a wonderful, almost buttery-sweet flavor that is enhanced when roasted. Place ½ cup whole hazelnuts on a baking sheet and roast them in a 300°F oven for 10 to 15 minutes. Wait until the nuts cool and rub them between your hands to remove the skins. Chop and store the nuts in a

sealed container in the cupboard for up to 1 week.

Nutrition: Calories: 296 Total Fat: 12g Protein: 2g Cholesterol: 0mg Sodium: 70mg Carbohydrates: 41g Fiber: 1g

214. Sun-dried Tomato Pesto Snapper

Preparation Time: 5 minutes

Cooking Time: 15 minutes

Servings: 4

Ingredients:

- 1 sweet onion, cut into ¼-inch slices
- 4 (5-ounce) snapper fillets
- Freshly ground black pepper, for seasoning
- ¼ cup sun-dried tomato pesto
- 2 tablespoons finely chopped fresh basil

Directions:

1. Preheat the oven to 400°F. Put parchment paper in a baking dish and arrange the onion slices on the bottom.
2. Pat the snapper fillets dry with a paper towel and season them lightly with pepper.
3. Place the fillets on the onions and spread 1 tablespoon of pesto on each fillet.
4. Bake until the fish flakes easily with a fork, 12 to 15 minutes.
5. Serve topped with basil.

Nutrition: Calories: 199 Total Fat: 3g Protein: 36g Cholesterol: 66mg Sodium: 119mg Carbohydrates: 3g Fiber: 1g

215. Trout-Cilantro Packets

Preparation Time: 5 minutes

Cooking Time: 20 minutes

Servings: 4

Ingredients:

- 4 cups cauliflower florets
- 2 red bell peppers
- 2 cups snow peas, stringed
- 4 (5-ounce) trout fillets
- Sea salt, for seasoning
- Freshly ground black pepper, for seasoning
- 2 tablespoons olive oil
- 2 tablespoons finely chopped cilantro

Directions:

1. Preheat the oven to 400°F.
2. Prepare four pieces of aluminum foil, each 12 inches square.
3. Evenly divide the cauliflower, bell peppers, and snow peas between the pieces of foil.
4. Pat dry the trout fillets with paper towels. Season them with salt and pepper.
5. Place a fillet on each foil square and drizzle the olive oil over the fish.
6. Fold the foil up to form tightly sealed packets and put them on a baking sheet.

7. Bake until cooked for about 20 minutes.

8. Serve topped with cilantro.

Nutrition: Calories: 398 Total Fat: 23g Saturated Fat: 5g Protein: 35g Cholesterol: 80mg Sodium: 153mg Carbohydrates: 16g Fiber: 6g

216.   Soused Herring

Preparation Time: 10 minutes

Cooking Time: 30 minutes

Servings: 4

Ingredients:

- 4 whole herring fillets, scaled, filleted, and trimmed

- 2 cups water

- ½ sweet onion, thinly sliced

- ½ cup white vinegar

- 2 thyme sprigs

- 1 tablespoon granulated sugar

- 1 teaspoon sea salt

- ¼ teaspoon black peppercorns

Directions:

1. Preheat the oven to 350°F.

2. Place the herring fillets in a 9-by-13-inch baking dish.

3. Add the water, onion, white vinegar, thyme, sugar, salt, and peppercorns.

4. Cover baking dish with foil. Bake the fish until tender for 25 to 30 minutes.

5. Cool before serving. This can be stored resealable container for 1 week.

Nutrition: Calories: 277 Total Fat: 15g Protein: 29g Cholesterol: 96mg Sodium: 482mg Carbohydrates: 5g; Fiber: 15g

217.   Traditional Succotash

Preparation Time: 10 minutes

Cooking Time: 20 minutes

Servings: 4

Ingredients:

- 2 tablespoons olive oil

- 1 sweet onion, finely chopped

- 1 tablespoon minced garlic

- 2 (15-ounce) cans diced sodium-free tomatoes, undrained

- 2 cups shelled edamame

- 2 cups corn

- 1 orange bell pepper, seeded and diced

- Sea salt, for seasoning

- Freshly ground black pepper, for seasoning

- 2 tablespoons fresh parsley, for garnish

Directions:

1. Using a large skillet, pour olive oil, then put it on a medium-high heat.

2. Sauté the onion and garlic until softened, about 3 minutes.

3. Add the tomatoes, edamame, corn, and bell pepper.

4. Make sure it boils, then reduce the heat to low and simmer until the vegetables are tender, about 15 minutes.

5. Season with salt and pepper.

6. Serve topped with parsley.

Nutrition: Calories: 265 Total Fat: 12g Protein: 11g Cholesterol: 0mg Sodium: 101mg Carbohydrates: 27g Fiber: 6g

218. Black-Eyed Pea Kale Bowl

Preparation Time: 10 minutes

Cooking Time: 20 minutes

Servings: 4

Ingredients:

- ½ cup brown rice
- 1 tablespoon olive oil
- ½ sweet onion, finely chopped
- 2 teaspoons minced garlic
- 2 (15-ounce) cans black peas
- 4 cups fresh kale
- 2 large tomatoes, finely chopped
- 3 tablespoons finely chopped chives

Directions:

1. Cook the rice and set aside. You can do this up to 3 days ahead, storing the rice in a sealed container in the refrigerator.

2. Pour on olive oil in a skillet and set it on medium-high heat.

3. Sauté the onion and garlic until softened, about 3 minutes.

4. Stir in the black-eyed peas and rice and cook until heated through, about 10 minutes.

5. Stir in the kale and sauté until wilted for five minutes.

6. Distribute mixture into 4 bowls and divide tomatoes between the bowls.

7. Serve topped with chives.

Nutrition: Calories: 257 Total Fat: 6g Protein: 13g Cholesterol: 0mg Sodium: 73mg Carbohydrates: 42g Fiber: 10g

219. Pumpkin Garam Masala

Preparation Time: 10 minutes

Cooking Time: 30 minutes

Servings: 4

Ingredients:

- 2 tablespoons olive oil
- 1 sweet onion, finely chopped
- 2 teaspoons minced garlic
- 4 cups diced fresh or frozen pumpkin
- 2 (15-ounce) cans white kidney beans, drained and rinsed
- 2 tomatoes, diced
- 1 cup low-sodium vegetable stock
- 2 tablespoons garam masala spice

Directions:

1. In a saucepan, put olive oil, then turn it in medium-high heat.

2. Sauté the onion and garlic until softened, about 3 minutes.

3. Stir in the pumpkin, beans, tomatoes, vegetable stock, and garam masala.

4. Bring the curry to boil and then reduce the heat to low and simmer until the pumpkin is tender, about 25 minutes.

Nutrition: Calories: 235 Total Fat: 8g Protein: 12g Cholesterol: 0mg Sodium: 17mg Carbohydrates: 33g Fiber: 8g

220. Spicy Tomato Braised Chickpeas

Preparation Time: 10 minutes

Cooking Time: 20 minutes

Servings: 4

Ingredients:

- 1 tablespoon olive oil
- 1 sweet onion, finely chopped
- 1 tablespoon minced garlic
- 2 (15-ounce) cans crushed tomatoes
- 2 (15-ounce) cans chickpeas, drained and rinsed
- ½ cup finely chopped fresh basil
- ⅛ Teaspoon red pepper flakes
- Sea salt, for seasoning
- Freshly ground black pepper, for seasoning
- 3 zucchini, spiralized

Directions:

1. Prepare, then heat the olive oil in a saucepan in medium-high heat.
2. Sauté the onion and garlic until softened, about 3 minutes.
3. Stir in the tomatoes, chickpeas, basil, and red pepper flakes.

4. Reduce to low heat if the sauce is already boiling, then simmer for 10 minutes to reduce the liquid slightly.
5. Season the sauce with salt and pepper.
6. Serve over spiralized zucchini.

Nutrition: Calories: 415 Total Fat: 6g Protein: 18g Cholesterol: 0mg Sodium: 215mg Carbohydrates: 74g Fiber: 18g

221. Baked Zucchini Chips

Preparation Time: 10 minutes

Cooking Time: 2 hours and 45 minutes

Servings: 10

Ingredients:

- 2 medium zucchini, sliced with a mandolin
- 1 tablespoon olive oil
- 1/2 teaspoon salt

Directions:

1. Preheat your oven to 200 degrees F.
2. Prepare a parchment paper and line it with the baking sheets.
3. Mix every ingredient in the large bowl and toss to thoroughly coat the zucchini with oil and salt.
4. Single later the zucchini slices on the baking sheet. It should not overlap.
5. Bake it in the oven for 2 and a half hours or until the zucchini chips are golden and crispy.
6. Turn the off oven, then allow it to cool with the oven door slightly open.

7. This will allow the zucchini chips to crisp up even more as they cool.

Nutrition: Fat: 1.5g Carbohydrates: 1.3g Protein: 0.5g

222. 5-Ingredient Ice-cream

Preparation Time: 10 minutes

Cooking Time: 1 hour 10 minutes

Servings: 6

Ingredients:

- 1 ½ cup full fat coconut milk
- ⅓ Cup natural peanut butter
- 2 tablespoons vanilla extract
- ⅛ Teaspoon stevia powder
- A pinch of salt

Directions:

1. Prior to starting this recipe, place a freezer-safe container in the freezer for at least 24 hours before to ensure that when the ice cream mixture is transferred no ice crystals are formed.

2. Blend all the ingredients and blend until a smooth and creamy consistency is achieved.

3. Chill this mixture by placing it in the refrigerator for 1 hour.

4. Transfer the mixture to an ice-cream maker and churn for 10 minutes or until it achieves a soft serve consistency.

5. Transfer the ice cream to the prepared freezer-safe container and freeze for at least one hour before serving. Can be served with caramel sauce.

Nutrition: Fat: 10.1g Carbohydrates: 3.7 Protein: 4.7g

223. Peanut Butter Cups

Preparation Time: 10 minutes

Cooking Time: 45 minutes

Servings: 18

Ingredients:

- ½ cup peanut butter
- 1 cup sugar-free dark chocolate chips
- 1 tablespoon coconut oil

Directions:

1. Get a microwave-safe bowl and place all the chocolate chips and coconut oil in the bowl. Microwave in 15 second bursts to melt the chocolate. Stir to combine the two ingredients.

2. Put a spoonful of chocolate into foil candy cups. Swirl so that the chocolate coats the sides of the cups. Pour excess chocolate back into the bowl.

3. Place the chocolate lined cups in the freezer for 10 minutes or until chocolate is set.

4. While the chocolate is setting, place the peanut butter in a microwave-safe bowl and microwave in 15 second bursts until the peanut butter becomes pourable.

5. Pour a spoonful of peanut butter into each of the chocolate-set cups. Make sure that the cup is a flat surface to smooth the tops of the peanut butter.

6. Pour a tablespoon of melted chocolate on top of the peanut butter in each cup.

7. Place it in the freezer for about 10 minutes to set chocolate. Unmold and serve. This can be stored using an airtight container and refrigerate for up to 3 days, or you can make it last in the freezer for a month.

8. Put it in the freezer for at least 10 minutes to set the chocolate. Then serve. Using an airtight container, you can refrigerate it for up to 3 days.

Nutrition: Fat: 5.7g Carbohydrates: 3.2g Protein: 2g

224. <u>Spiced Kale Chips</u>

Preparation Time: 10 minutes

Cooking Time: 30 minutes

Servings: 4

Ingredients:

- 1 bunch curly kale
- 1 tablespoon olive oil
- ¼ teaspoon of salt
- ⅛ Teaspoon garlic powder
- ⅛ Teaspoon black pepper

Directions:

1. Preheat the oven to 300 degrees F.

2. Prepare an aluminum foil and line it in a baking sheet pan.

3. Rinse and dry kale thoroughly by spinning in a salad spinner or patting it with paper towels.

4. Tear kale leaves off the stems and break into pieces the size of potato chips. Place into a large mixing bowl and add the rest of the ingredients. Toss so that the kale leaves are thoroughly coated with the spices and oil.

5. Place the coated kale leaves in an even layer that does not overlap on a wire baking rack. Place the wire baking rack atop the foil lined baking sheet.

6. Bake it for 20 minutes or wait until the kale leaves are crispy.

7. Allow to cool and serve.

Nutrition: Fat: 3g Carbohydrates: 1.8g Protein: 0.9g

225. <u>Coconut Fat Cups</u>

Preparation Time: 10 minutes

Cooking Time: 15 minutes

Servings: 10

Ingredients:

- ¼ cup coconut butter, melted
- ¼ cup coconut oil, melted
- 3 drops liquid stevia
- ⅓ Cup shredded coconut

Directions:

1. Mix the ingredients in a medium bowl and thoroughly combine.

2. Using a tablespoon, fill mini cupcake liners or an ice cube tray with the mixture.

3. Freeze for at least 1 hour and serve. Using an airtight container, you can refrigerate it for up until 2 days.

Nutrition: Fat: 11.7g Carbohydrates: 2.5g Protein: 0.7g

226. Raw Strawberry Crumble

Preparation Time: 10 minutes

Cooking Time: 5 minutes

Servings: 6

Ingredients:

- 4 cups fresh strawberries, hulled and sliced
- ¼ cup unsweetened coconut flakes
- ½ cup raw walnuts
- ½ tbsp. Ginger, grated
- ½ tbsp. ground cinnamon

Directions:

1. Arrange sliced strawberries on the bottom of a pie dish or serving bowls.
2. Add all of the rest of the ingredients to a food processor and pulse until a crumble consistency is.
3. Arrange the crumble on top of the strawberries and serve.

Nutrition: Fat: 15.7g Carbohydrates: 6.1g Protein: 13.1g

227. Peanut Butter Energy Bars

Preparation Time: 10 minutes

Cooking Time: 10 minutes

Servings: 8

Ingredients:

- 1 cup smooth peanut butter
- 4 teaspoons granulated erythritol
- ⅓ cup coconut flour
- 2 tablespoons water

Directions:

1. Get a 9-inch loaf pan and put a parchment paper.
2. Mix erythritol, peanut butter, and water in a medium bowl until a smooth consistency is achieved.
3. Stir in coconut flour and blend well to make a very thick but not dry mixture. If the mixture appears dry, add a few more teaspoons of water.
4. Press mixture into prepared loaf pan.
5. Put it in the refrigerator for at least 2 hours until set firm.
6. Remove the chilled bars from the loaf pan and cut them into bars. Serve. Can be stored in a tight container to refrigerate it up to 1 month or up to 6 months in the freezer.

Nutrition: Fat: 17g Carbohydrates: 13.8g Protein: 9.1g

228. Sunflower Parmesan "Cheese"

Preparation Time: 5 minutes

Cooking Time: 25 minutes

Servings: 4

Ingredients:

- ½ cup sunflower seeds
- 2 tablespoons nutritional yeast
- ½ teaspoon garlic powder

Directions:

1. Combine the sunflower seeds, nutritional yeast, and garlic powder in a food processor or blender. Process on low for 30 to 45 seconds, or until

the sunflower seeds have been broken down into a chunk- like.

2. Store in a refrigerator-safe container for up to 2 months.

Nutrition: Calories: 56 Total fat: 4g Carbohydrates: 3g Fiber: 1g Protein: 3g

229.   **Banana Peanut Butter Yogurt Bowl**

Preparation Time: 5 minutes

Cooking Time: 0 minutes

Servings: 4

Ingredients:

- 1 teaspoon nutmeg
- ¼ Creamy peanut butter
- 2 medium-sized sliced bananas
- 4 cups vanilla flavor - Soy yogurt

Directions:

1. Divide the yogurt among four bowls and top with the slices of bananas. Soften the microwave in the microwave for forty seconds and then put one tablespoon into each bowl, then garnish with the nutmeg and flaxseed meal.

Nutrition: Calories 292 Fat 15g Carbs 24g Protein 29g Fiber 3g

230.   **Peanut Butter Fudge**

Preparation Time: 30 minutes

Cooking Time: 0 minutes

Servings: 20

Ingredients:

- 1 teaspoon vanilla extract

- 3 tablespoons maple syrup
- ½ cup coconut oil
- 1 cup creamy peanut butter
- 2 cups coconut flakes, unsweetened

Directions:

1. Use spray oil on an eight-inch square pan. Cream the shredded coconut in a food processor until it forms a buttery substance. Put the coconut butter into a bowl and blend in the coconut oil and peanut butter. Then add in the vanilla and mix once more. Spoon the mix into the pan and let it set.

Nutrition: Calories 164 Protein 4g Fiber 2g Carbs 5g Fat 16g

231.   **Roasted Chickpeas**

Preparation Time: 5 minutes

Cooking Time: 30 minutes

Servings: 4

Ingredients:

- 1 (14.5-ounce) can chickpeas, drained but not rinsed
- 1 teaspoon extra-virgin olive oil or 2 teaspoons reserved chickpea brine
- 1 teaspoon smoked paprika
- 1 teaspoon garlic powder

Directions:

1. Preheat the oven to 425°F. Line a baking sheet with parchment paper.

2. After draining the chickpeas, pat dry with a paper towel. Transfer to a medium bowl. Add the olive oil, paprika, and garlic powder. Using a

wooden spoon or your hands, toss gently to coat.

3. Spread the chickpeas out on the prepared baking sheet in a single layer. Roast for 30 minutes, rotating the baking sheet after 15 minutes.

4. Turn the oven off, open the oven door about five inches, and allow the chickpeas to cool in the oven. Transfer all of the chickpeas into a glass pint jar or divide evenly among 4 (4-ounce) jelly jars. Cool completely before closing tightly with lids.

Nutrition: Calories: 157 Total fat: 3g Carbohydrates: 28g Fiber: 6g Protein: 6g

232. Tamari Almonds

Preparation Time: 5 minutes

Cooking Time: 15 minutes

Servings: 8

Ingredients:

- 1 pound raw almonds
- 3 tablespoons tamari or soy sauce
- 2 tablespoons extra-virgin olive oil
- 1 tablespoon nutritional yeast
- 1 to 2 teaspoons chili powder, to taste

Directions:

1. Preheat the oven to 400°F. Line a baking sheet with parchment paper.

2. In a medium bowl, combine the almonds, tamari, and olive oil until well coated. Spread the almonds on the prepared baking sheet and roast for 10 to 15 minutes until browned.

3. Cool for 10 minutes, then season with the nutritional yeast and chili powder.

4. Transfer to a glass jar and close tightly with a lid.

Nutrition: Calories: 364 Total fat: 32g Carbohydrates: 13g Fiber: 6g Protein: 13g

233. Taco Pita Pizzas

Preparation Time: 5 minutes

Cooking Time: 7 minutes

Servings: 4

Ingredients:

- 4 sandwich-size pita bread pieces or Sandwich Thins
- 1 cup vegetarian refried beans
- 1 cup pizza sauce
- 1 cup chopped mushrooms
- 1 teaspoon minced jalapeño (optional)

Directions:

1. Preheat the oven to 400°F. Line a large baking sheet with parchment paper.

2. Assemble 4 pizzas: On each pita, spread about ¼ cup of refried beans. Pour ¼ cup of pizza sauce over the beans and spread evenly. Add ¼ cup of mushrooms. Sprinkle ¼ teaspoon of minced jalapeño (if using) over the mushrooms.

3. Place the pizzas on the prepared baking sheet and bake for 7 minutes.

4. Cool completely before placing each pizza in a freezer-safe plastic bag, or store together in one large airtight,

freezer-safe container with parchment paper between the pizzas.

Nutrition: Calories: 148 Total fat: 2g Carbohydrates: 29g Fiber: 5g Protein: 6g

234. Risotto Bites

Preparation Time: 15 minutes

Cooking Time: 20 minutes

Servings: 12 bites

Ingredients:

- ½ cup panko bread crumbs
- 1 teaspoon paprika
- 1 teaspoon chipotle powder or ground cayenne pepper
- 1½ cups cold Green Pea Risotto
- Nonstick cooking spray

Directions:

1. Preheat the oven to 425°F. Line a baking sheet with parchment paper.
2. On a large plate, combine the panko, paprika, and chipotle powder. Set aside.
3. Roll 2 tablespoons of the risotto into a ball. Gently roll in the bread crumbs and place on the prepared baking sheet. Repeat to make a total of 12 balls.
4. Spritz the tops of the risotto bites with nonstick cooking spray and bake for 15 to 20 minutes, until they begin to brown.
5. Cool completely before storing in a large airtight container in a single layer (add a piece of parchment paper for a

second layer) or in a plastic freezer bag.

Nutrition: Calories: 100 Total fat: 2g Carbohydrates: 17g Fiber: 5g Protein: 6g

235. Healthy Protein Bars

Preparation Time: 19 minutes

Cooking Time: 0 minutes

Servings: 12 balls

Ingredients:

- 1 large banana
- 1 cup of rolled oats
- 1 serving of vegan vanilla protein powder

Directions:

1. Using your food processor, blend the protein powder, and rolled oats.
2. Blend them for 1 minute until you have a semi-coarse mixture. The oats should be slightly chopped, but not powdered.
3. Add the banana and form a pliable and coarse dough.
4. Shape into either balls or small bars and store them in a container.
5. Eat one and store the rest in an airtight container in the refrigerator!

Nutrition: Fat 0.7 g Carbohydrates 8 g Protein- 2.7 g Calories: 47

236. Quick Peanut Butter Bars

Preparation Time: 10 minutes

Cooking Time: 0 minutes

Servings: 10

Ingredients:

- 20 soft-pitted Medjool dates
- 1 cup of raw almonds
- 1 ¼ cup of crushed pretzels
- 1/3 cup of natural peanut butter

Directions:

1. Transfer your almonds to a food processor and mix them until they are broken.

2. Add the peanut butter and the dates. Blend them until you have a thick dough

3. Crush the pretzels and put them in the processor. Pulse enough to mix them with the rest of the ingredients. You can also give them a good stir with a spoon.

4. Take a small, square pan and line it with parchment paper. Press the dough onto the pan, flattening it with your hands or a spoon.

5. Put it in the freezer for about 2 hours or in the fridge for about 4 hours.

6. Once it is fully set, cut it into bars. Store them and enjoy them when you are hungry.

7. Just remember to store them in a sealed container.

Nutrition: Calories: 343 Fat 23 g Carbohydrates 33 g Protein 5 g

237. Hummus without Oil

Preparation Time: 5 minutes

Cooking Time: 0 minutes

Servings: 6

Ingredients:

- 2 tablespoons of lemon juice
- 1 15-ounce can of chickpeas
- 2 tablespoons of tahini
- 1-2 freshly chopped/minced garlic cloves
- Red pepper hummus
- 2 tablespoons of almond milk pepper

Directions:

1. Wash with running water the chickpeas and put them in a high-speed blender with garlic. Blend them until they break into fine pieces.

2. Add the other ingredients and blend everything until you have a smooth paste. Add some water if you want a less thick consistency.

3. Your homemade hummus dip is ready to be served with eatables

Nutrition: Calories: 202 Fat 3 g Carbohydrates 35 g Protein 11 g

CHAPTER 7:

JUICES AND SMOOTHIES RECIPES

238. Mango Smoothie

Preparation Time: 3 minutes

Cooking Time: 0 minutes

Servings: 2

Ingredients:

- 2 fresh mangoes
- 1 frozen banana
- 1/2 cup milk
- 1/2 cup yogurt
- ⅛ Cup unsweetened coconut

Directions:

1. Put everything into the blender until the desired consistency is achieved. Enjoy immediately!

Nutrition: Calories: 329.6 Carbohydrates: 64.5g Protein: 6.3g Fat: 8.6g Sodium: 27.7mg Fiber: 7.2g Sugar: 53.1g

239. Beetroot Smoothie

Preparation Time: 4 minutes

Cooking Time: 0 minutes

Servings: 1

Ingredients:

- ½ apple (e.g., Golden Delicious)
- 1 small beetroot, pre-cooked
- ½ lime (juiced)
- 1 tsp. maple syrup
- 10 mint, fresh, and 1¼ cups water

Directions:

1. Put everything into the blender. Enjoy!

Directions: Calories: 95 Fat: 1g Cholesterol: 2mg Carbohydrates: 19g Fiber: 4g Sugar: 13g Protein: 4g

240. Avocado Smoothie

Preparation Time: 5 minutes

Cooking Time: 0 minutes

Servings: 2

Ingredients:

- ½ avocado
- 3 celery stalks
- 1 lime
- Fresh mint leaves
- 1 tsp. linseeds

Directions:

1. Put everything into the blender. Enjoy!
2. Better when it's cool, you can keep the smoothie in the refrigerator for 1 to 2 days in an airtight container.

Nutrition: Calories: 178 Sugar: 8g Sodium: 105mg Fat: 11.6g Saturated fat: 2.1g Carbohydrates: 19.3g Fiber: 5.7g Protein: 2.5g

241. Red Smoothie

Preparation Time: 5 minutes

Cooking Time: 0 minutes

Servings: 1

Ingredients:

- 2 cups mixed frozen red berries such as strawberries and raspberries
- 1 small red beet, peeled and thinly sliced

- 1 tablespoon fresh lemon juice
- 1 tablespoon honey
- 2 teaspoons unrefined extra-virgin coconut oil

Directions:

1. Put everything into the blender until the desired consistency is achieved. Enjoy immediately!

Nutrition: Calories: 221 Fat: 1g Cholesterol: 0mg Sodium: 10mg Carbohydrates: 56g Fiber: 12g Sugar: 33g Protein: 3g

242. Kale Smoothie

Preparation Time: 3 minutes

Cooking Time: 0 minutes

Servings: 1

Ingredients:

- 2 cups of kale leaves
- 1 cup of almond milk
- 1 banana
- 1 apple
- Cinnamon

Directions:

1. Put everything into the blender. Enjoy!
2. You may need a lid and scrape the blender walls to blend everything together. Pour into a glass and serve immediately!

Nutrition: Calories: 187 Fat: 9g Cholesterol: 3mg Sodium: 149mg Carbohydrates: 27g Fiber: 4g Sugar: 13g Protein: 8g

243. Melon Smoothie

Preparation Time: 5 minutes

Cooking Time: 0 minutes

Servings: 2

Ingredients:

- 1/4 cantaloupe - peeled, seeded, and cubed
- 1/4 honeydew melon - peeled, seeded, and cubed
- 1 lime, juiced
- 3 fresh mint leaves
- 2 tablespoons sugar

Directions:

1. Combine cantaloupe, honeydew, lime juice, and sugar in a blender. Blend until smooth. Pour into glasses and serve.

Nutrition: Calories: 70 Fat: 0.2g Carbohydrates: 18.1g Protein: 0.8g Cholesterol: 0mg Sodium: 20mg

244. Pineapple Smoothie

Preparation Time: 5 minutes

Cooking Time: 0 minutes

Servings: 2

Ingredients:

- ½ cup of fresh pineapple
- ½ cup of strawberry
- 1 banana
- ¼ cup of orange juice
- Mint ice cubes

Directions:

1. Place the pineapple juice, banana, frozen pineapple, and vanilla Greek yogurt in a blender.

2. Blend until smooth.

3. Pour into 2 glasses. Garnish with pineapple wedges and mint sprigs if desired.

Directions: Calories: 169 Carbohydrates: 33g Protein: 6g Cholesterol: 2mg Sodium: 33mg Fiber: 7g Sugar: 35g

245. Sweet Smoothie

Preparation Time: 5 minutes

Cooking Time: 0 minutes

Servings: 2

Ingredients:

- 1 banana
- 1 sliced mango
- 1 cup fresh pineapple
- 1 tablespoon peanut butter
- ½ coconut water

Directions:

1. Process the banana, mango, pineapple, peanut butter, and coconut water in a blender until smooth and creamy.

2. Enjoy immediately or keep cool in the refrigerator.

Nutrition: Calories: 168 Fat: 0.7g Carbohydrates: 42.3g Protein: 1.5g Cholesterol: 0mg Sodium: 5mg

246. Strawberry-Flax Smoothie

Preparation Time: 5 minutes

Cooking Time: 0 minutes

Servings: 1

Ingredients:

- 1 cup of frozen strawberries
- ¾ cup plain low-fat yogurt
- ½ cup fresh orange juice
- 1 tablespoon honey
- 1 tablespoon flaxseed meal

Directions:

1. Combine the strawberries, yogurt, orange juice, honey, and flaxseed meal in a blender.

2. Blend until smooth.

Nutrition: Calories: 334 Fat: 7g Cholesterol: 11mg, Sodium: 134mg Protein: 14g Carbohydrate: 58g Sugar: 49g Fiber: 6g

247. Coconut Milk Smoothie

Preparation Time: 5 minutes

Cooking Time: 0 minutes

Servings: 4

Ingredients:

- 1 10-ounce frozen blueberries
- 1 cup plain yogurt
- 3 ripe bananas
- 1 cup unsweetened coconut milk
- 2 tablespoons honey

Directions:

1. Combine the blueberries, bananas, yogurt, coconut milk, and honey in a blender and serve.

Nutrition: Calories: 300 Fat: 15g Cholesterol: 10mg Sodium: 40mg Carbohydrate: 43g Fiber: 3g Sugar: 28g Protein: 5g

248. Spiced Pumpkin Smoothie

Preparation Time: 5 minutes

Cooking Time: 0 minutes

Servings: 1

Ingredients:

- 1 cup ice
- ½ cup whole milk
- ⅓ Cup pure pumpkin puree
- 1 tablespoon honey
- Pinch of ground nutmeg

Directions:

1. Place the ice, milk, pumpkin puree, honey, and nutmeg in a blender.
2. Blend until smooth.

Nutrition: Calories: 165 Fat: 4g Cholesterol: 12mg Sodium: 53mg Protein: 5g Carbohydrate: 29g Sugar: 26g Fiber: 3g

249. Carrot-Pineapple Smoothie

Preparation Time: 5 minutes

Cooking Time: 0 minutes

Servings: 2

Ingredients:

- ¾ cup chopped fresh pineapple
- ½ cup ice
- ⅓ Cup fresh orange juice
- ¼ cup chopped carrot
- ½ banana

Directions:

1. Place the pineapple, ice, orange juice, carrot, and banana in a blender.
2. Blend until smooth.

Nutrition: Calories: 159 Fat: 1g Cholesterol: 0mg Sodium: 25mg Protein: 2g Carbohydrate: 40g Sugar: 26g Fiber: 4g

250. Groovy Green Smoothie

Preparation Time: 10 minutes

Cooking Time: 0 minutes

Servings: 2

Ingredients:

- 1 banana, cut in chunks
- 1 cup grapes
- 1 (6 ounces) tub vanilla yogurt
- 1/2 apple, cored and chopped
- 1 1/2 cups fresh spinach leaves

Directions:

1. Put the banana, grapes, yogurt, apple, and spinach in a blender. Cover and mix until smooth.
2. Pour into glasses and serve.

Nutrition: Calories 205 Fat 1.9g Carbohydrates 45g Protein 6.1g Cholesterol 4mg Sodium 76mg

251. Sun Juice

Preparation Time: 10 minutes

Cooking Time: 0 minutes

Servings: 1

Ingredients:

- 2 oranges, peeled and sliced
- 1/2 cup fresh raspberries
- 1 medium-sized banana, peeled
- 3 fresh mint leaves

Directions:

1. Juice everything in the juice machine. Pour on the ice to serve.

Nutrition: Calories 293 Fat 1.1g Carbohydrates 73.6g Protein 5g Cholesterol 0mg

252. Protein-Packed Blueberry Smoothie

Preparation Time: 5 minutes

Cooking Time: 0 minutes

Servings: 2

Ingredients:

- ¾ unsweetened coconut milk
- ½ cup unsweetened almond milk
- ⅓ Cup frozen blueberries
- 4 tablespoons vanilla protein powder

Directions:

1. Put everything into the blender until a smooth consistency is achieved. Serve and enjoy!

Nutrition: Fat: 6.1g Carbohydrates: 6g Protein: 6.4g

253. Strawberry Protein Smoothie

Preparation Time: 5 minutes

Cooking Time: 0 minutes

Servings: 2

Ingredients:

- ½ cup frozen strawberries
- 1 tablespoon almond butter
- ½ scoop vanilla protein powder
- ⅓ Cup almond milk
- ½ cup ice

Directions:

1. Put everything into the blender. Serve and enjoy!

Nutrition: Fat: 14.2g Carbohydrates: 7.5g Protein: 8.4g

254. Raspberry Avocado Smoothie

Preparation Time: 5 minutes

Cooking Time: 0 minutes

Servings: 2

Ingredients:

- 1 small ripe avocado, peeled and pitted
- ¼ cup raspberries, frozen
- 2 tablespoons lemon juice
- 1 cup water

Directions:

1. Put everything into the blender until a smooth consistency is achieved. Serve and enjoy!

Nutrition: Fat: 19.8g Carbohydrates: 10.8g Protein: 2.2g

255. Easy Antioxidant Smoothie

Preparation Time: 3 minutes

Cooking Time: 0 minutes

Servings: 2

Ingredients:

- 2-3 frozen broccoli florets
- 1 cup orange juice
- 2 plums, cut
- 1 cup raspberries
- 1 tsp. ginger powder

Directions:

1. Combine all ingredients in a high-speed blender and blend until smooth.

Nutrition: Calories: 150 Carbohydrates: 36g Total fat: 1g Protein: 1g

256. Healthy Purple Smoothie

Preparation Time: 3 minutes

Cooking Time: 0 minutes

Servings: 2

Ingredients:

- 2-3 frozen broccoli florets
- 1 cup water
- 1/2 avocado, peeled and chopped
- 3 plums, chopped
- 1 cup blueberries

Directions:

1. Combine all ingredients in a high-speed blender and blend until smooth.

Nutrition: Calories: 45 Carbohydrates: 3g Total fat: 2g Protein: 1g

257. Mom's Favourite Kale Smoothie

Preparation Time: 3 minutes

Cooking Time: 0 minutes

Servings: 2

Ingredients:

- 2-3 ice cubes
- 1½ cup orange juice
- 1 green small apple, cut
- ½ cucumber, chopped
- 2-3 leaves kale
- ½ cup raspberries

Directions:

1. Combine all ingredients in a high-speed blender and blend until smooth.

Nutrition: Calories: 51 Carbohydrates: 0g Total fat: 0g Protein: 0g

258. Creamy Green Smoothie

Preparation Time: 3 minutes

Cooking Time: 0 minutes

Servings: 2

Ingredients:

- 1 frozen banana
- 1 cup coconut milk
- 1 small pear, chopped
- 1 cup baby spinach
- 1 tsp. vanilla extract

Directions:

1. Combine all ingredients in a high-speed blender and blend until smooth.

Nutrition: Calories: 301 Carbohydrates: 21g Total fat: 9g Protein: 29g

259. Strawberry and Arugula Smoothie

Preparation Time: 3 minutes

Cooking Time: 0 minutes

Servings: 2

Ingredients:

- 2 cups frozen strawberries
- 1 cup unsweetened almond milk
- 10-12 arugula leaves
- 1/2 tsp. ground cinnamon

Directions:

1. Combine ice, almond milk, strawberries, arugula, and cinnamon in a high-speed blender. Blend until smooth and serve.

Nutrition: Calories: 2 Carbohydrates: 0g Total fat: 0g Protein: 0g

260. Emma's Amazing Smoothie

Preparation Time: 3 minutes

Cooking Time: 0 minutes

Servings: 2

Ingredients:

- 1 frozen banana, chopped
- 1 cup orange juice
- 1 large nectarine, sliced

- 1/2 zucchini, peeled and chopped
- 2-3 dates, pitted

Directions:

1. Combine all ingredients in a high-speed blender and blend until smooth.

Nutrition: Calories: 2 Carbohydrates: 0g Total fat: 0g Protein: 0g

261. Good-To-Go Morning Smoothie

Preparation Time: 3 minutes

Cooking Time: 0 minutes

Servings: 2

Ingredients:

- 1 cup frozen strawberries
- 1 cup apple juice
- 1 banana, chopped
- 1 cup raw asparagus, chopped
- 1 tbsp. ground flaxseed

Directions:

1. Combine all ingredients in a high-speed blender and blend until smooth.

Nutrition: Calories: 200 Carbohydrates: 25g Total fat: 0g Protein: 2g

262. Endless Energy Smoothie

Preparation Time: 3 minutes

Cooking Time: 0 minutes

Servings: 2

Ingredients:

- 1 frozen banana, chopped
- 11/2 cup green tea

- 1 cup chopped pineapple
- 1 lime, juiced
- 1 tbsp. chia seeds

Directions:

1. Combine all ingredients in a high-speed blender and blend until smooth.

Nutrition: Calories: 49 Carbohydrates: 11g Total fat: 0g Protein: 0g

263. High-fibre Fruit Smoothie

Preparation Time: 3 minutes

Cooking Time: 0 minutes

Servings: 2

Ingredients:

- 1 frozen banana, chopped
- 1 cup orange juice
- 2 cups chopped papaya
- 1 cup shredded cabbage
- 1 tbsp. chia seeds

Directions:

1. Combine all ingredients in a high-speed blender and blend until smooth.

Nutrition: Calories: 168 Carbohydrates: 26g Total fat: 3g Protein: 6g

264. Nutritious Green Smoothie

Preparation Time: 3 minutes

Cooking Time: 0 minutes

Servings: 2

Ingredients:

- 2-3 frozen broccoli florets
- 1 cup apple juice

- 1 large pear, chopped
- 1 kiwi, peeled and chopped
- 1 cup spinach leaves

Directions:

1. Combine all ingredients in a high-speed blender and blend until smooth.

Nutrition: Calories: 44 Carbohydrates: 0g Total fat: 0g Protein: 0g

265. Apricot, Strawberry, and Banana Smoothie

Preparation Time: 3 minutes

Cooking Time: 0 minutes

Servings: 2

Ingredients:

- 1 frozen banana
- 11/2 cup almond milk
- 5 dried apricots
- 1 cup fresh strawberries

Directions:

1. Combine all ingredients in a high-speed blender and blend until smooth.

Nutrition: Calories: 69 Carbohydrates: 17g Total fat: 0g Protein: 1g

266. Spinach and Green Apple Smoothie

Preparation Time: 3 minutes

Cooking Time: 0 minutes

Servings: 2

Ingredients:

- 3-4 ice cubes

- 1 cup unsweetened almond milk
- 1 banana, peeled and chopped
- 2 green apples, peeled and chopped
- 1 cup raw spinach leaves
- 3-4 dates, pitted

Directions:

1. Combine all ingredients in a high-speed blender and blend until smooth.

Nutrition: Calories: 249 Carbohydrates: 46g Total fat: 3g Protein: 9g

267. Super food Blueberry Smoothie

Preparation Time: 3 minutes

Cooking Time: 0 minutes

Servings: 2

Ingredients:

- 2-3 cubes frozen spinach
- 1 cup green tea
- 1 banana
- 2 cups blueberries
- 1 tbsp. ground flaxseed

Directions:

1. Combine all ingredients in a high-speed blender and blend until smooth.

Nutrition: Calories: 249 Carbohydrates: 46g Total fat: 3g Protein: 9g

268. Zucchini and Blueberry Smoothie

Preparation Time: 3 minutes

Cooking Time: 0 minutes

Servings: 2

Ingredients:

- 1 cup frozen blueberries
- 1 cup unsweetened almond milk
- 1 banana
- 1 zucchini, peeled and chopped

Directions:

1. Combine all ingredients in a high-speed blender and blend until smooth.

Nutrition: Calories: 244 Carbohydrates: 19g Total fat: 4g Protein: 20g

269. Tropical Spinach Smoothie

Preparation Time: 3 minutes

Cooking Time: 0 minutes

Servings: 2

Ingredients:

- 1/2 cup crushed ice or 3-4 ice cubes
- 1 cup coconut milk
- 1 mango, peeled and diced
- 1 cup fresh spinach leaves
- 4-5 dates, pitted
- 1/2 tsp. vanilla extract

Directions:

1. Combine all ingredients in a high-speed blender and blend until smooth.

Nutrition: Calories: 130 Carbohydrates: 26g Total fat: 0g Protein: 1g

270. Peach Grapefruit Ginger Smoothie

Preparation Time: 5 minutes

Cooking Time: 0 minutes

Servings: 2

Ingredients:

- ½ frozen banana
- 1 teaspoon of fresh mint, chopped
- 1 cup frozen peaches
- 1 teaspoon ground ginger
- 1 cup grapefruit juice

Directions:

1. Blend well in the blender, slowly at first, and then increasing the speed to break down the fruit and blend it well.

Nutrition: Calories: 187 Carbohydrates: 32g Total fat: 2g Protein: 13g

271. Great Green Smoothie

Preparation Time: 5 minutes

Cooking Time: 0 minutes

Servings: 4

Ingredients:

- 4 bananas, peeled
- 4 cups hulled strawberries
- 4 cups spinach
- 4 cups plant-based milk

Directions:

1. Open 4 quart-size, freezer-safe bags. In each, layer in the following order: 1 banana (halved or sliced), 1 cup of strawberries, and 1 cup of spinach. Seal and place in the freezer.

2. To serve, take a frozen bag of Great Green Smoothie ingredients and transfer it to a blender. Add 1 cup of plant-based milk and blend until smooth.

Nutrition: Calories: 173 Carbohydrates: 40g Total fat: 2g Protein: 4g

272. Blueberry and Sweet Potato Smoothie

Preparation time: 5 minutes

Cooking time: 0 minutes

Servings: 1

Ingredients:

- 1/4 cup frozen blueberries
- 1/2 cup frozen sweet potato, cooked
- 1/8 teaspoon sea salt
- 1 tablespoon cacao powder
- 1 scoop of chocolate protein powder
- 1 cup almond milk

Directions:

1. Place all the ingredients in the order in a food processor or blender and then pulse for 2 to 3 minutes at high speed until smooth.

2. Pour the smoothie into a glass and then serve.

Nutrition: Calories: 150.7 Fat: 2.9 g Carbs: 27 g Protein: 7.4 g

273. Peanut Butter and Coffee Smoothie

Preparation time: 5 minutes

Cooking time: 0 minutes

Servings: 1

Ingredients:

- Small frozen banana
- 1/2 teaspoon ground turmeric
- 1 Tablespoon chia seeds
- Scoop of chocolate protein powder
- Tablespoons Peanut Butter
- Cup strong coffee, brewed

Directions:

1. Place all the ingredients in the order in a food processor or blender and then pulse for 2 to 3 minutes at high speed until smooth.

2. Pour the smoothie into a glass and then serve.

Nutrition: Calories: 189 Fat: 7 g Carbs: 24.5 g Protein: 10.3 g

274. Beet and Orange Smoothie

Preparation time: 5 minutes

Cooking time: 0 minutes

Servings: 1

Ingredients:

- 1 Cup chopped zucchini rounds, frozen
- 1 cup spinach
- 1 small peeled navel orange, frozen
- 1 small chopped beet

- 1 scoop of vanilla protein powder
- 1 cup almond milk, unsweetened

Directions:

1. Place all the ingredients in the order in a food processor or blender and then pulse for 2 to 3 minutes at high speed until smooth.

2. Pour the smoothie into a glass and then serve.

Nutrition: Calories: 253 Cal Fat: 5 g Carbs: 44.6 g Protein: 3 g

275. Strawberry, Banana, and Coconut Shake

Preparation time: 5 minutes

Cooking time: 0 minutes

Servings: 1

Ingredients:

- 1 tablespoon coconut flakes
- 1/2 cups frozen banana slices
- 1 strawberries, sliced
- 1/2 cup coconut milk, unsweetened
- 1/4 cup strawberries for topping

Directions:

1. Place all the ingredients in the order in a food processor or blender, except for topping, and then pulse for 2 to 3 minutes at high speed until smooth.

2. Pour the smoothie into a glass and then serve.

Nutrition: Calories: 335 Fat: 5 g Carbs: 75 g Protein: 4 g

276. Green Colada

Preparation time: 5 minutes

Cooking time: 0 minutes

Servings: 1

Ingredients:

- 1/2 cup frozen pineapple chunks
- 1/2 banana
- 1/2 teaspoon spirulina powder
- 1/4 teaspoon vanilla extract, unsweetened
- 1 cup of coconut milk

Directions:

1. Place all the ingredients in the order in a food processor or blender and then pulse for 2 to 3 minutes at high speed until smooth. Pour the smoothie into a glass and then serve.

Nutrition: Calories: 127 Fat: 3 g Carbs: 25 g Protein: 3 g

277. Avocado Spinach Smoothie

Preparation Time: 5 minutes

Cooking Time: 5 minutes

Servings: 2

Ingredients Coconut milk: 1 cup

- Frozen banana: 1 small sliced
- Avocado: 1 small
- Baby spinach: 1 ½ cup

Directions:

1. Add all the ingredients to the blender
2. Blend to form a smooth consistency

Nutrition Carbs: 29.2 g Protein: 9.2 g Fats: 10.3 g Calories: 235

278. Almond Spinach Smoothie

Preparation Time: 15 minutes

Cooking Time: 5 minutes

Servings: 1

Ingredients Large banana: 1 - Ice cubes: 4

- Almonds: ¼ cup
- Fresh spinach: 1 cup
- Rolled oats: 2 tbsp.
- Unsweetened almond milk: ¾ cup

Directions:

1. Add all the ingredients to the blender
2. Blend to form a smooth consistency

Nutrition Carbs: 49.2 g Protein: 11.9 g Fats: 19.9 g Calories: 406

279. 3-Ingredient Mango Smoothie

Preparation Time: 15 minutes

Cooking Time: 5 minutes

Servings: 1

Ingredients

- Frozen mango chunks: 1 cup
- Oat milk: ½ cup
- Frozen banana: 1 large sliced

Directions:

1. Add all the ingredients to the blender
2. Blend until smooth

Nutrition Carbs: 67.1 g Protein: 3.5 g Fats: 1.7 g Calories: 276

CHAPTER 8:

OTHER RECIPES

280. Tahini Miso Dressing

Preparation Time: 10 minutes

Cooking Time: 0 minutes

Servings: 2

Ingredients:

- ¼ cup tahini
- 1 tablespoon tamari or low-sodium soy sauce
- 1 tablespoon white miso
- 1 tablespoon freshly squeezed lemon juice
- 1 tablespoon maple syrup or honey
- ¼ cup warm water
- Freshly ground black pepper

Directions:

1. In a small bowl, whisk the tahini, tamari, miso, lemon juice, and maple syrup together. Whisk in the water and black pepper. Store in an airtight container in the refrigerator for up to six months.

Nutrition: Calories: 76 Fat: 6g Carbs: 5g Protein: 2g

281. Balsamic Roasted Tomatoes

Preparation Time: 10 minutes

Cooking Time: 4 hours

Servings: 6

Ingredients:

- 6 medium tomatoes or 1 pint cherry tomatoes
- ¼ cup, plus 1 tablespoon olive oil
- Kosher salt

- Freshly ground black pepper
- 2 teaspoons balsamic vinegar

Directions:

1. Preheat the oven to 300°F. Put your rimmed baking sheet with parchment paper.
2. Wash and dry the tomatoes, and halve them crosswise. Put them cut-side up on the parchment paper, and drizzle them with ¼ cup of olive oil, allowing the oil to pool on the parchment paper. Sprinkle with salt and pepper.
3. Roast for 3 to 4 hours, or until the edges of the tomatoes are puckered, and the cut surface is a little dry.
4. Sprinkle with the balsamic vinegar and let cool on the baking sheet.
5. Pack into an airtight container and pour any excess oil from the parchment paper on top. Add the remaining 1 tablespoon of oil to the container. Seal and refrigerate for up to one month.

Nutrition: Calories: 123 Fat: 12g Carbs: 5g Protein: 1g

282. Crispy Spicy Chickpeas

Preparation Time: 5 minutes

Cooking Time: 30 minutes

Servings: 1

Ingredients:

- 1 cup canned chickpeas, drained and rinsed
- 1 tablespoon olive oil
- ½ teaspoon kosher salt

- ⅛ Teaspoon freshly ground black pepper
- ½ teaspoon smoked paprika
- ⅛ Teaspoon cayenne pepper

Directions:

1. Preheat the oven to 400°F.

2. Remove any remaining moisture from the chickpeas by rolling them between two paper towels. Place in a medium bowl.

3. Add the olive oil, salt, and pepper to the bowl and toss to completely coat the chickpeas.

4. Spread them out on a baking sheet. Roast for 20 minutes, stir, and roast for an additional 10 minutes, or until lightly crisped.

5. When it's still warm, toss the chickpeas with the smoked paprika and cayenne pepper. Adding the spices last prevents them from charring in the oven and provides a crispier chickpea.

6. You can keep it at room temperature in an open container for several days. This keeps them crisper longer, although they'll start to lose some crispness over time. They can also be stored in the refrigerator once they've completely cooled.

Nutrition: Calories: 101 Fat: 4g Carbs: 14g Protein: 3g

283. **Roasted Pumpkin Seeds**

Preparation Time: 5 minutes

Cooking Time: 10 minutes

Servings: 1

Ingredients:

- 1 cup unsalted pumpkin seeds
- 1 teaspoon olive oil
- ¼ teaspoon kosher salt
- Pinch cayenne pepper
- Pinch smoked paprika

Directions:

1. Using a small bowl, combine all of the ingredients.

2. Heat a small sauté pan over medium-low heat. Add the pumpkin seeds and sauté, tossing frequently as they brown, for 10 minutes, or until they reach your preferred level of toasting.

3. Cool and store at room temperature in an airtight container for up to two months or in the refrigerator for up to one year.

Nutrition: Calories: 20 Fat: 1g Carbs: 2g Protein: 1g

284. **Lemony Breadcrumbs**

Preparation Time: 5 minutes

Cooking Time: 10 minutes

Servings: 1

Ingredients:

- 2 teaspoons olive oil
- 1 cup panko
- ⅛ Teaspoon kosher salt

- ⅛ Teaspoon freshly ground black pepper
- Zest of 1 lemon (about ½ teaspoon or more, to taste)

Directions:

1. Using a small skillet over a medium heat, warm the olive oil. Add the panko, salt, and pepper. Toss to lightly coat and toast until the breadcrumbs are a golden color, about 3 minutes. You'll need to stir the breadcrumbs about every 30 seconds, so they toast evenly.

2. Take it out from the heat and stir in the lemon zest.

3. Transfer to a plate to cool before storing in an airtight container.

Nutrition: Calories: 63 Fat: 2g Carbs: 10g Protein: 2g

285. Cauliflower Skillet Steaks

Preparation Time: 15 minutes

Cooking Time: 15 minutes

Servings: 4

Ingredients:

- 1 large head cauliflower, sliced into 6 (1-inch-thick) steaks
- 2 tablespoons olive oil, divided
- ½ teaspoon smoked paprika
- ½ teaspoon kosher salt
- ¼ teaspoon cayenne pepper
- Balsamic Roasted Tomatoes

Directions:

1. Rub both sides of the cauliflower steaks lightly with 1 tablespoon of olive oil, and sprinkle on both sides with the paprika, salt, and cayenne.

2. Heat the remaining 1 tablespoon of olive oil in a large sauté pan over medium-high heat. Arrange the cauliflower steaks in the pan, including any extra florets. You need to cook the steaks in two batches.

3. Cook the cauliflower until slightly crisped, about 3 minutes per side. Reduce the heat to medium and continue to cook for another 8 to 10 minutes, or until the cauliflower is tender when pierced with a sharp knife.

4. Serve the cauliflower steaks topped with the roasted tomatoes.

Nutrition: Calories: 114 Fat: 8g Carbs: 11g Protein: 4g

286. Lemony Kale, Avocado, And Chickpea Salad

Preparation Time: 20 minutes

Cooking Time: 0 minutes

Servings: 4

Ingredients:

- 1 avocado, halved
- 2 tablespoons freshly squeezed lemon juice, divided
- ½ teaspoon kosher salt, divided
- 1 bunch curly kale, stems removed and discarded, leaves coarsely chopped (about 8 cups)

- 1 (15-ounce) can chickpeas, drained and rinsed
- 2 tablespoons extra-virgin olive oil
- ¼ teaspoon freshly ground black pepper
- ¼ cup Roasted Pumpkin Seeds or store-bought

Direction:

1. Slice your avocado, then coop its flesh from one of the avocado halves out of its skin and put it in a large bowl. Put a 1 tablespoon of lemon juice and ¼ teaspoon of salt and mash everything together. Add the coarsely chopped kale leaves and massage them by hand with the avocado mash until the kale becomes tender. Place the kale-avocado mash on a serving plate.

2. Remove the flesh of the remaining avocado half from its skin and chop into bite-size chunks. Place in the bowl that contained the kale and add the chickpeas.

3. In a small bowl, whisk together the olive oil, the remaining 1 tablespoon of lemon juice, the remaining ¼ teaspoon of salt, and the pepper. Drizzle over the chickpeas and avocado and toss to combine. Pile on top of the kale-avocado mash and top with the roasted pumpkin seeds.

Nutrition: Calories: 383 Fat: 20g Carbs: 43g Protein: 14g

287.   Lentil Potato Salad

Preparation Time: 10 minutes

Cooking Time: 25 minutes

Servings: 2

Ingredients:

- ½ cup beluga lentils
- 8 fingerling potatoes
- 1 cup thinly sliced scallions
- ¼ cup halved cherry tomatoes
- ¼ cup Lemon Vinaigrette
- Kosher salt, to taste
- Freshly ground black pepper, to taste

Directions:

1. Pour 2 cups of water to simmer in a small pot and add the lentils. Cover and simmer for 20 to 25 minutes, or until the lentils are tender. Drain and set aside to cool.

2. While the lentils are cooking, bring a medium pot of well-salted water to a boil and add the potatoes. Low heat to simmer and cook for about 15 minutes, or until the potatoes are tender. Drain. Once cool enough to handle, slice, or halve the potatoes.

3. Place the lentils on a serving plate and top with the potatoes, scallions, and tomatoes. Drizzle with the vinaigrette and season with salt and pepper.

Nutrition: Calories: 400 Fat: 26g Carbs: 39g Protein: 7g

288. Curried Apple Chips

Preparation Time: 15 minutes

Cooking Time: 1 hour and 30 minutes

Servings: 25 chips

Ingredients:

- 1 tablespoon freshly squeezed lemon juice
- ½ cup water
- 2 apples, such as Fuji or Honey crisp, cored and thinly sliced into rings
- 1 teaspoon curry powder

Directions:

1. Preheat the oven to 200°F.Put a rimmed baking sheet with parchment paper.

2. Mix the lemon juice and water together in a medium bowl. As soon as the apples are sliced, add them to the bowl to soak for 2 minutes. Drain and pat dry with paper towels. Arrange in a single layer on the baking sheet.

3. Place the curry powder in a sieve or other sifter and lightly sprinkle the apple slices. Not too much curry goes a long way, so it's okay not to dust both sides of the apple rings.

4. In you preheated oven, bake it for 45 minutes. After 45 minutes, turn the slices over and bake for another 45 minutes, again without opening the oven. If you find the apple chips need additional crisping, bake for another 15 minutes.

5. For the crispiest texture, let the chips cool before eating, but they're pretty fabulous slightly warm.

Nutrition: Calories: 61 Fat: 0g Carbs: 16g Protein: 0g

289. Bok Choy–Asparagus Salad

Preparation Time: 20 minutes

Cooking Time: 0 minutes

Servings: 4

Ingredients:

- 4 cups coarsely chopped baby bok Choy
- 1½ cups asparagus, trimmed and cut into 1½-inch lengths
- 1 cup cauliflower rice
- 1 cup strawberries, chopped into bite-size chunks
- 1 mango, peeled and diced
- ½ cup scallions, sliced into 1-inch lengths - ¼ cup Lemon Vinaigrette

Directions:

1. In a large bowl, combine the bok choy, asparagus, cauliflower rice, strawberries, mango, and scallions. Drizzle with the vinaigrette and gently toss.

Nutrition: Calories: 210 Fat: 14g Carbs: 21g Protein: 3g

290. Lemony Romaine and Avocado Salad

Preparation Time: 15 minutes

Cooking Time: 0 minutes

Servings: 6

Ingredients: 1 head romaine lettuce

- ½ cup pomegranate seeds

- ¼ cup pine nuts
- ¼ cup Lemon Vinaigrette
- 2 avocados
- Freshly ground black pepper

Directions:

1. Wash your vegetables and spin-dry, then slice the leaves into bite-size pieces. Transfer the leaves to a large bowl, and toss with the pomegranate seeds, pine nuts, and half of the vinaigrette.

2. Slice the avocados in half. Remove the pit from each and slice the avocados into long thin slices. Using a large spoon, carefully scoop the slices out of the peel.

3. Arrange your avocado slices on top of the lettuce in the bowl and drizzle half of the remaining dressing over them. Carefully toss using your hands or a large metal spoon. Add the remaining dressing as needed.

4. Finish with a few sprinkles of pepper.

Nutrition: Calories: 217 Fat: 20g Carbs: 11g Protein 3g

291. <u>Strawberry-Coconut Smoothie</u>

Preparation Time: 10 minutes

Cooking Time: 0 minutes

Servings: 1

Ingredients:

- Dairy-free and Vegan: Use coconut milk yogurt

- 1 cup frozen strawberries, slightly thawed
- 1 very ripe banana, sliced and frozen
- ½ cup light coconut milk
- ½ cup plain Greek yogurt
- 1 teaspoon freshly squeezed lime juice
- 1 tablespoon chia seeds (optional)
- 3 or 4 ice cubes

Directions:

1. Transfer all your ingredients to a blender and blend until smooth. If necessary, add additional coconut milk or water to thin the smoothie to your preferred consistency.

Nutrition: Calories: 278 Fat: 2g Carbs: 57g Protein: 14g

292. <u>Aloha Mango-Pineapple Smoothie</u>

Preparation Time: 10 minutes

Cooking Time: 0 minutes

Servings: 2

Ingredients:

- 1 large navel orange, peeled and quartered
- 1 cup frozen pineapple chunks
- 1 cup frozen mango chunks
- 1 tablespoon freshly squeezed lime juice - ½ cup plain Greek yogurt
- ½ cup milk or coconut milk
- 1 tablespoon chia seeds (optional)
- 3 or 4 ice cubes

Directions:

1. Transfer all your ingredients in a blender and blend until smooth. If necessary, add additional milk or water to thin the smoothie to your preferred consistency.

Nutrition: Calories: 158 Fat: 1g Carbs: 35g Protein: 7g

293. Lentil Soup

Preparation Time: 15 Minutes

Cooking Time: 25 Minutes

Servings: 4

Ingredients:

- 1 tbsp. Olive Oil
- 4 cups Vegetable Stock
- 1 Onion, finely chopped
- 2 Carrots, medium
- 1 cup Lentils, dried
- 1 tsp. Cumin

Directions:

1. To make this healthy soup, first, you need to heat the oil in a medium-sized skillet over medium heat.
2. Once the oil becomes hot, stir in the cumin and then the onions.
3. Sauté those for 3 minutes or until the onion is slightly transparent and cooked.
4. To this, add the carrots and toss them well.
5. Next, stir in the lentils. Mix well.

6. Now, pour in the vegetable stock and give a good stir until everything comes together.
7. As the soup mixture starts to boil, reduce the heat and allow it to simmer for 10 minutes while keeping the pan covered.
8. Turn off the heat and then transfer the mixture to a bowl.
9. Finally, blend it with an immersion blender or in a high-speed blender for 1 minute or until you get a rich, smooth mixture.
10. Serve it hot and enjoy.

Nutrition: Calories: 251 Kcal Protein: 14g Carbohydrates: 41.3g Fat: 4.1g

294. Trail Mix

Preparation Time: 10 Minutes

Cooking Time: 10 Minutes

Servings: 2

Ingredients:

- 1 cup Walnuts, raw
- 2 cups Tart Cherries, dried
- 1 cup Pumpkin Seeds, raw
- 1 cup Almonds, raw
- ½ cup Vegan Dark Chocolate
- 1 cup Cashew

Directions:

1. First, mix all the ingredients needed to make the trail mix in a large mixing bowl until combined well.

2. Store in an air-tight container.

Nutrition: Calories: 596 Kcal Protein: 17.5g Carbohydrates: 46.1g Fat: 39.5g

295.   Flax Crackers

Preparation Time: 5 Minutes

Cooking Time: 60 Minutes

Servings: 4 to 6

Ingredients:

- 1 cup Flaxseeds, whole
- 2 cups Water
- ¾ cup Flaxseeds, grounded
- 1 tsp. Sea Salt
- ½ cup Chia Seeds
- 1 tsp. Black Pepper
- ½ cup Sunflower Seeds

Directions:

1. Using a large bowl, you need to put all your ingredients, then mix them well. Soak them in with water for about 10 to 15 minutes.

2. After that, transfer the mixture to a parchment paper-lined baking sheet and spread it evenly. Tip: Make sure the paper lines the edges as well.

3. Next, bake it for 60 minutes at 350 °F.

4. Once the time is up, flip the entire bar and take off the parchment paper.

5. Bake for half an hour or until it becomes crispy and browned.

6. Allow it to cool completely and then break it down.

Nutrition: Calories: 251cal Proteins: 9.2g Carbohydrates: 14.9g Fat: 16g

296.   Crunchy Granola

Preparation Time: 10 Minutes

Cooking Time: 20 Minutes

Servings: 1

Ingredients:

- ½ cup Oats
- Dash of Salt
- 2 tbsp. Vegetable Oil
- 3 tbsp. Maple Syrup
- 1/3 cup Apple Cider Vinegar
- ½ cup Almonds
- 1 tsp. Cardamom, grounded

Directions:

1. Preheat the oven to 375 °F.

2. After that, mix oats, pistachios, salt, and cardamom in a large bowl.

3. Next, spoon in the vegetable oil and maple syrup to the mixture.

4. Then, transfer the mixture to a parchment-paper-lined baking sheet.

5. Bake them for 13 minutes or until the mixture is toasted. Tip: Check on them now and then. Spread it out well.

6. Return the sheet to the oven for ten minutes.

7. From your oven, remove the sheet and allow it to cool completely.

8. Serve and enjoy.

Nutrition: Calories: 763Kcal Proteins: 12.9g Carbohydrates: 64.8g Fat: 52.4g

297. Chickpea Scramble Bowl

Preparation Time: 10 Minutes

Cooking Time: 10 Minutes

Servings: Makes 2 Bowl

Ingredients:

- ¼ of 1 Onion, diced
- 15 oz. Chickpeas
- 2 Garlic cloves, minced
- ½ tsp. Turmeric
- ½ tsp. Black Pepper
- ½ tsp. Extra Virgin Olive Oil
- ½ tsp. Salt

Directions:

1. Begin by placing the chickpeas in a large bowl along with a bit of water.
2. Soak for few minutes and then mash the chickpeas lightly with a fork while leaving some of them in the whole form.
3. Next, spoon in the turmeric, pepper, and salt to the bowl. Mix well.
4. Then, heat oil in a medium-sized skillet over medium-high heat.
5. Once the oil becomes hot, stir in the onions.
6. Sauté the onions for 3 to 4 minutes or until softened.
7. Then, add the garlic and cook for 1 minute or until aromatic.
8. After that, stir in the mashed chickpeas. Cook for another 4 minutes or until thickened.
9. Serve along with micro greens. Place the greens at the bottom, followed by the scramble, and top it with cilantro or parsley.

Nutrition: Calories: 801Kcal Proteins: 41.5g Carbohydrates: 131.6g Fat: 14.7g

298. Maple Flavoured Oatmeal

Preparation Time: 5 Minutes

Cooking Time: 25 Minutes

Servings: 2

Ingredients:

- 2 tbsp. Maple Syrup
- 1 cup Oatmeal
- ½ tsp. Cinnamon
- 2 ½ cup Water
- 2/3 cup Soy Milk
- 1 tsp. Earth Balance or Vegan Butter

Directions:

1. To start with, place oatmeal and water in a medium-sized saucepan over medium-high heat.
2. Bring the mixture to a boil.
3. Next, lower the heat and cook for 13 to 15 minutes while keeping the pan covered. Tip: At this point, all the water should get absorbed by the grains.
4. Now, remove the pan from the heat and fluff this mixture with a fork.
5. Cover the pan again. Set it aside for 5 minutes.
6. Then, stir in all the remaining ingredients to the oatmeal mixture until everything comes together.

7. Serve and enjoy.

Nutrition: Calories: 411Kcal Proteins: 14.7g Carbohydrates: 73.6g Fat: 6.6g

299. Protein Pancakes

Preparation Time: 5 Minutes

Cooking Time: 10 Minutes

Servings: Makes 6 Pancakes

Ingredients:

- 1 cup All-Purpose Flour
- 2 tbsp. Maple Syrup
- ¼ cup Brown Rice Protein Powder
- ½ tsp. Sea Salt
- 1 tbsp. Baking Powder
- 1 cup Water

Directions:

1. To make these delightful protein-rich pancakes, you first need to combine the flour, sea salt, baking powder, and vegan protein powder in a large mixing bowl.

2. Spoon in the maple syrup and then later gradually add the water until you get a thick and lumpy batter.

3. Now, heat a non-stick pan over medium-high heat.

4. Then, scoop a ladle of the batter into it and cook the pancakes for 2 to 3 minutes or until bubbles form.

5. Cook each side for a further minute.

6. Serve immediately.

Nutrition: Calories: 295 Kcal Protein: 15.8g Carbohydrates: 59.9g Fat: 1.2g

300. Squash Lentil Soup

Preparation Time: 10 Minutes

Cooking Time: 35 Minutes

Servings: 4

Ingredients:

- 7 cups Vegetable Broth
- 2 tbsp. Olive Oil
- 2 tsp., Sage dried
- 1 Yellow Onion, medium & diced.
- Salt & Pepper to taste
- 1 Butternut Squash
- 1 ½ cup Red Lentils

Directions:

1. Using a saucepan, start heating your oil and stir in the onions.

2. Sauté the onions for 2 to 3 minutes or until softened.

3. Once cooked, stir in squash and sage while stirring continuously.

4. Then, spoon in the lentils, salt, and pepper.

5. Bring the lentil mixture to a boil for about 30 minutes. Lower the heat.

6. Then, allow the soup to cool down until the lentils are soft.

7. Finally, transfer the mixture to a high-speed blender and blend for 3 to 4 minutes or until smooth.

8. Serve hot.

Nutrition: Calories: 421 Kcal Protein: 16.7g Carbohydrates: 51g Fat: 4.5g

301. Sweet Potato Gnocchi

Preparation Time: 30 minutes

Cooking Time: 30 minutes

Servings: 2

Ingredients

- 2 cups flour
- ¼ teaspoon salt
- ½ teaspoon turmeric
- 3 garlic cloves, roasted
- 1 sweet potato

Directions

1. To begin this recipe, you will want to heat your oven to 375°f. Once the oven is warm, place the sweet potato on a baking sheet and pop it in for thirty minutes.

2. During the last five minutes of the bake time, add the garlic cloves into the oven and allow them to roast.

3. When the time is up, remove the baking sheet from the oven and allow the ingredients to cool for ten minutes or so.

4. Next, you will want to remove the skin of the sweet potato. Once this is done, place the sweet potato into a mixing bowl and add in the garlic. Carefully take a fork and mash everything together until there are no chunks.

5. At this point, you can season the sweet potato with turmeric and salt.

6. With the sweet potato now seasoned, it is time to add the flour. You will want to add the flour in half of a cup at a time.

7. Be sure to stir the ingredients together well before you add any more flour. The amount of flour may vary depending on the size of the sweet potato. You will want to continue adding flour until it becomes difficult to stir.

8. Now, your sweet potato should have a dough-like consistency. Break the dough up and roll the sweet potato into strips.

9. Using a knife, you can cut these strips into half-inch pieces.

10. Once you have finished making your gnocchi, you will want to take a large pot of water and bring it to a boil over high heat.

11. When your water is boiling carefully drop in the gnocchi pieces.

12. When they are cooked through, the pieces will rise to the top. Typically, this will take two to three minutes. Enjoy!

Nutrition: Calories: 460 Fat: 5 g Carbs: 45 g Protein: 10 g

302. Taco Pasta Bowl

Preparation Time: 10 minutes

Cooking Time: 30 minutes

Servings: 4

Ingredients:

- 1 can black beans
- 1 cup corn
- ½ cup diced onion
- 1 jar salsa
- 1 box pasta

- ¼ teaspoon cumin
- 2 tablespoons chili powder

Directions:

1. To start, please cook the pasta of your choice according to the directions provided on the box. Once this step is complete, you can drain the water and set the pasta to the side.

2. Next, you will want to take a medium pan and place it over medium to high heat. Add one tablespoon of your oil and bring it to sizzle. Once the oil is hot, place your onion and cook for three to five minutes. By the end, the onion should be soft.

3. At this point, you will add in the beans, corn, salsa, and spices. I have chosen to use chili powder and cumin, but you can spice your dish however you would like!

4. Last, you will pour your sauce over your pasta and enjoy!

Nutrition: Calories: 480 Fat: 8 g Carbs: 46 g Protein: 18 g

303. **Vegan BBQ Tofu**

Preparation Time: 10 minutes

Cooking Time: 40 minutes

Servings: 3

Ingredients:

- ¼ cup vegan BBQ sauce
- ¼ teaspoon pepper
- ¼ teaspoon garlic powder
- ¼ teaspoon salt
- 1 tablespoon grapeseed oil

- 1 pack firm tofu

Directions:

1. Before you begin cooking your tofu, you will want to press it. Generally, this will take thirty to forty-five minutes. If possible, try to press the tofu overnight so that it is ready for you when you need it.

2. Once your tofu is ready, bring a saucepan over medium heat and allow it to warm up. As your saucepan is warming up, slice your tofu into small pieces. Put a 1 tablespoon of oil and spread your tofu across the pan. At this point, season your tofu and cook for five minutes. Be sure to flip each piece of tofu until it is a nice golden-brown color all over.

3. Finally, remove the tofu from the pan and cover it in BBQ sauce. This meal is excellent alone or with your favorite grain or vegetable.

Nutrition: Calories: 290, Fat: 64 g, Carbs: 25 g, Protein: 20 g

304. **Mustard Tomato Mix**

Preparation time: 10 minutes

Cooking time: 10 minutes

Servings: 4

Ingredients:

- 2 pounds plum tomatoes, sliced
- A pinch of salt and black pepper
- 2 tablespoons avocado oil
- 3 tablespoons lime juice
- 1 tablespoon Dijon mustard

- 1 tablespoon mint, chopped

Directions:

1. Using a pan, heat your oil over medium heat, add the tomatoes, the lime juice, and the other ingredients, toss, cook for 10 minutes, divide between plates and serve.

Nutrition: Calories: 120 Fat: 4 g Carbs: 15 g Protein: 6 g

305. Veggies and noodle bowl with mushrooms

Preparation Time: 10 minutes

Cooking Time: 20 minutes

Servings: 2

Ingredients:

- 8 ounces sliced mushrooms
- 9 oz. rinsed and sliced leeks
- 8 ounces noodles
- 5 ounces baby spinach

Directions:

1. Boil the noodles according to the given directions on the packet, remove the boiling water, rinse with cold water, and set aside.

2. Now take a bowl, add all the ingredients, and whisk them well until all the ingredients are combined well.

Nutrition: Calories: 260 Fat: 4 g Carbs: 35 g Protein: 4 g

306. Broccoli over Orzo

Preparation Time: 10 minutes

Cooking Time: 25 minutes

Servings: 3

Ingredients:

- 3 teaspoons olive oil
- 4 garlic cloves, smashed
- 2 cups broccoli florets
- 4½ ounces orzo pasta
- ¼ teaspoon salt
- ¼ teaspoon pepper

Directions:

1. Start off by preparing your broccoli. You can do this by trimming the stems off and slicing the broccoli into small, bite-size pieces. If you want, go ahead and season with salt.

2. Next, you will want to steam your broccoli over a little bit of water until it is cooked through. Once the broccoli is cooked, chop it up into even smaller pieces.

3. When the broccoli is done, cook your pasta according to the directions provided on the box. Once this is done, drain the water and then place the pasta back into the pot.

4. With the pasta and broccoli done, place it back into the pot with the garlic. Stir everything together well and cook until the garlic turns a nice golden color. Be sure to stir everything to combine your meal well. Serve warm and enjoy a simple dinner!

Nutrition: Calories: 310 Fat: 4 g Carbs: 35 g Protein: 10 g

307. Mango Pineapple Hoisin Sauce

Preparation Time: 10 minutes

Cooking Time: 10 minutes

Servings: 2

Ingredients:

- 1 ½ cups fresh mango juice or pureed mango
- ⅔ cup vegan hoisin sauce
- 4 tablespoons brown rice vinegar
- 1 cup fresh pineapple juice
- ½ cup tamari or soy sauce
- 2 tablespoons Sriracha sauce

Directions:

1. Use a pan and heat oil over medium heat.
2. Add all the ingredients and stir constantly.
3. Simmer until the mixture thickens.

Nutrition: Calories: 125 Fat: 2 g Carbs: 8 g Protein: 4.3 g

308. Sriracha Sauce

Preparation Time: 20 minutes

Cooking Time: 10 minutes

Servings: 2

Ingredients

- 15 red Fresno chilies, chopped into chunks
- ½ tablespoon salt
- 4 garlic cloves
- ¼ cup apple cider or white vinegar
- 2 tablespoons raw sugar

Directions:

1. Place the chilies, garlic, salt, and sugar into a food processor. Pulse until coarsely chopped. Transfer into a mason's jar.
2. Cover with a plastic cling and leave it for 5-7 days to ferment. Stir often during this period. In 3-4 days you will see some bubbles appearing.
3. Transfer the contents of the jar into a blender. Add vinegar and blend until smooth.
4. Transfer into a saucepan after passing through a wire mesh strainer.
5. Bring to a boil on high heat.
6. When it starts boiling, reduce the heat and simmer for 5 minutes. Remove from heat and cool.
7. Transfer into a flip top bottle. Refrigerate until use.

Nutrition: Calories: 90 Fat: 6 g Carbs: 5 g Protein: 1 g

309. White Sauce (Béchamel)

Preparation Time: 10 minutes

Cooking Time: 12 minutes

Servings: 2

Ingredients:

- 6 tablespoons olive oil
- 4 cups soymilk or any other non-dairy milk of your choice
- 5 tablespoons all-purpose flour
- Sea salt to taste

- Black pepper to taste

Directions:

1. Place a heavy pot over a medium heat. Add oil. When the oil is heated, add sifted flour into the pan. Stir constantly for about a minute. It will begin to change color; be careful not to burn it!

2. Pour in the milk, stirring constantly. Keep stirring until thick.

3. Simmer until the thickness you desire is nearly achieved. This is because the sauce thickens further as it cools.

4. Turn off the heat. Add salt, pepper, and any other herbs and spices if you desire.

Nutrition: Calories: 68 Fat: 2 g Carbs: 1.5 g Protein: 5 g

310. Spinach & orange salad

Preparation Time: 15 minutes

Cooking Time: 0 minutes

Servings: 6

Ingredients

- ¼ -⅓ cup vegan dressing
- 3 oranges, medium, peeled, seeded & sectioned
- ¾ lb. spinach, fresh & torn
- 1 red onion, medium, sliced & separated into rings

Directions:

1. Toss everything together and serve with dressing.

Nutrition: Calories: 100 Fat: 2 g Carbs: 12 g Protein: 5 g

311. Lime-macerated mangos

Preparation Time: 10 minutes

Cooking Time: 0 minutes

Servings: 5

Ingredients: 3 ripe mangos

- ⅓ cup light brown sugar
- 2 tablespoons fresh lime juice
- ½ cup dry white wine
- Fresh mint sprigs

Directions

1. Peel, pit, and cut the mangos into 1/2-inch dice. Layer the diced mango in a large bowl, sprinkling each layer with about 1 tablespoon of the sugar. Cover with plastic wrap and refrigerate for 2 hours.

2. Pour in the lime juice and wine, mixing gently to combine with the mango. Cover and refrigerate for 4 hours.

3. About 30 minutes before serving time, bring the fruit to room temperature. To serve, spoon the mango and the liquid into serving glasses and garnish with mint.

Nutrition: Calories: 150 Fat: 2g Carbs: 16 g Protein: 8 g

312. Raspberry chia pudding

Preparation Time: 10 minutes

Cooking Time: 0 minutes

Servings: 2

Ingredients

- 4 tablespoons chia seeds

- 1 cup coconut milk
- ½ cup raspberries

Directions:

1. Add raspberry and coconut milk in a blender and blend until smooth.
2. Pour mixture into the Mason jar.
3. Add chia seeds in a jar and stir well.
4. Close the jar tightly with lid and shake well.
5. Place in the refrigerator for 3 hours.
6. Serve chilled and enjoy.

Nutrition: Calories: 140 Fat: 5 g Carbs: 20 g Protein: 8 g

313. Lemon Mousse

Preparation Time: 10 minutes + 2 hours

Cooking Time: 0 minutes

Servings: 2

Ingredients

- 14 oz. coconut milk
- 12 drops liquid stevia
- ½ tsp. lemon extract
- ¼ tsp. turmeric

Directions

1. Refrigerate a 1 can coconut milk overnight. Scoop out thick cream into a mixing bowl.
2. Add remaining ingredients to the bowl and whip using a hand mixer until smooth.
3. Transfer mousse mixture to a zip-lock bag and pipe into small serving glasses. Place in refrigerator.

4. Serve chilled and enjoy.

Nutrition: Calories: 200 Fat: 6 g Carbs: 28 g Protein: 8 g

314. Banana Mango Ice Cream

Preparation Time: 30 Minutes

Cook Time: 0 Minutes

Servings: 2

Ingredients:

- 1 banana, peeled and sliced
- 2 ripe mangos with the skin removed, and the flesh cubed
- 3 tablespoons almond or cashew milk, chilled

Directions:

1. Lay out the banana and mango slices on a baking sheet lined with parchment paper and place them in the freezer.
2. Once they are frozen solid, remove the fruit and place it in the food processor.
3. Add the cold milk and process until smooth, about three to four minutes.
4. Taste and add sweetener as needed.
5. Serve immediately.

Nutrition: Calories 306 Fat 6.8g Carbohydrate 65.1g Protein 3.9g

315. Raspberry Chia Pudding Shots

Preparation Time: 1 hour

Cook Time: 15 Minutes

Servings: 2

Ingredients:

- ¼ cup chia seeds
- ½ cup raspberries
- ½ cup coconut milk
- ¼ cup almond milk
- 1 Tbsps. cacao powder
- 1 Tbsps. stevia

Directions:

1. Combine all ingredients except raspberries in a jar.
2. Let sit for 2-3 minutes and transfer to shot glasses.
3. Refrigerate 1 hour or overnight to serve as breakfast.
4. Serve with fresh raspberries.

Nutrition: Calories 246 Fat 23.1g Carbohydrate 13.6g Protein 3.6g

316. Sautéed Bosc Pears with Walnuts

Preparation Time: 15 Minutes

Cook Time: 16 Minutes

Servings: 6

Ingredients:

- 2 Tbsps. salted butter
- ¼ tsp. cinnamon
- ¼ tsp. nutmeg, ground
- 6 Bosc pears, peeled, quartered
- 1 Tbsps. lemon juice
- ½ cup walnuts, chopped, toasted

Directions:

1. Melt butter in a skillet, add spices, and cook for 30 seconds.
2. Add pears and cook for 15 minutes. Stir in lemon juice.
3. Serve topped with walnuts.

Nutrition: Calories 221 Fat 10.3g Carbohydrate 33g Protein 3.3g

317. Mango & Papaya After-Chop

Preparation Time: 25 Minutes

Cook Time: 0 Minutes

Servings: 1

Ingredients:

- ¼ of papaya, chopped
- 1 mango, chopped
- 1 Tbsps. coconut milk
- ½ tsp. maple syrup
- 1 Tbsps. peanuts, chopped

Directions:

1. Cut open the papaya. Scoop out the seeds, chop.
2. Peel the mango. Slice the fruit from the pit, chop.
3. Put the fruit in a bowl. Add remaining ingredients. Stir to coat.

Nutrition: Calories 330 Fat 9.6g Carbohydrate 63.4g Protein 5.8g

318. Greek-style garbanzo beans

Preparation Time: 8 hours 5 minutes

Cook Time: 10 hours

Servings: 10

Ingredients:

- 12 ounces garbanzo beans
- 14 oz. tomatoes with juice, chopped
- 2 stalks celery, diced
- 1 onion, diced
- 4 garlic cloves, minced
- ¼ tsp. Salt

Directions:

1. Soak beans in water for 8 hours.
2. Combine drained beans with the remaining ingredients. Stir and pour water to cover.
3. Cook for 10 hours on low. Season with salt and serve.

Nutrition: Calories 138 Fat 2.2g Carbohydrate 23.7g Protein 7.1g

319. Butter Bean Hummus

Preparation Time 5 Minutes

Cook Time: 0 Minutes

Servings: 4

Ingredients:

- 1 can butter beans, drained, rinsed
- 2 garlic cloves, minced
- ½ lemon, juiced
- 1 Tbsps. olive oil
- 4 sprigs of parsley, minced
- ¼ tsp. Sea salt

Directions:

1. Blend all ingredients in a food processor into a creamy mixture.
2. Serve as a dip for bread, crackers, or any type of vegetables.

Nutrition: Calories 84 Fat 3.9g Carbohydrate 10.2g Protein 3.1g

320. Black Beans & Brown Rice

Preparation Time: 2 Minutes

Cook Time: 45 Minutes

Servings: 4

Ingredients:

- 4 cups water
- 2 cups brown rice, uncooked
- 1 can no-salt black beans
- 3 cloves garlic, minced

Directions:

1. Bring the water and rice to boil, simmer for 40 minutes.
2. In a pan, cook the black beans with their liquid and the garlic for 5 minutes.
3. Toss the rice and beans together, and serve.

Nutrition: Calories 429 Fat 3.3g Carbohydrate 87.3g Protein 12.5g

321.   Beans & Greens Bowl

Preparation Time: 2 Minutes

Cook Time: 2 Minutes

Servings: 1

Ingredients:

- 1½ cups curly kale, washed, chopped
- ½ cup black beans, cooked
- ½ avocado
- 2 Tbsps. feta cheese, crumbled

Directions:

1. Mix the kale and black beans in a microwavable bowl and heat for about 1 ½ minutes.
2. Add the avocado and stir well. Top with feta.

Nutrition: Calories 830 Fat 29.6g Carbohydrate 113.7g Protein 46.9g

322.   Millet and Teff with Squash & Onions

Preparation Time: 10 Minutes

Cook Time: 20 Minutes

Servings: 6

Ingredients:

- 1 cup millet
- ½ cup teff grain
- 4½ cups of water
- 1 onion, sliced
- 1 butternut squash, chopped
- ¼ tsp. Sea salt

Directions:

1. Rinse millet and put in a large pot.

2. Add remaining ingredients. Mix well.
3. Simmer 20 minutes until all the water is absorbed.
4. Serve hot.

Nutrition: Calories 218 Fat 1.7g Carbohydrate 45.2g Protein 6.6g

323.   Quesadilla with Black Beans and Sweet Potato

Preparation Time: 10 minutes

Cook Time: 30 minutes

Servings: 2

Ingredients:

- 1 medium-sized sweet potato, peeled and cut into cubes
- 3 teaspoons taco seasoning
- 4 whole-wheat tortillas
- ½ of a 15-ounce can of black beans, drained and rinsed

Directions:

1. Bring a large pot of water to boil and drop in the sweet potato.
2. Boil for 10 to 20 minutes or until soft.
3. Drain the sweet potato and put it in a bowl.
4. Add the taco seasoning and mash well.
5. To assemble the quesadilla, spread the sweet potato mixture on the tortilla.
6. Add the black beans and press them into the potato mixture.
7. Cover with another tortilla.
8. Heat a nonstick skillet over medium-high heat and lay the tortilla in it.

Toast on both sides and serve immediately.

Nutrition: Calories 520 Fat 3g Carbohydrate 99.8g Protein 26.9g

324. Meatless Chick Nuggets

Preparation Time: 10 minutes

Cook Time: 30 minutes

Servings: 8

Ingredients:

- 1 15.5-ounce can chickpeas, rinsed and drained
- ½ teaspoon garlic powder
- 1 teaspoon granulated onion
- 1 tablespoon nutritional yeast
- 1 tablespoon whole-wheat bread crumbs
- ½ cup panko bread crumbs

Directions:

1. Preheat the oven to 350 degrees Fahrenheit and cover a rimmed baking pan with parchment paper.
2. Place the drained chickpeas in a food processor and pulse four to five times.
3. Add the garlic powder, granulated onion, nutritional yeast, and the tablespoon of whole-wheat bread crumbs to the processor and process until you get a chunky, grainy mixture that sticks together.
4. Scoop out by teaspoonfuls and form balls.
5. Roll the balls in the panko crumbs and set them on the baking sheet, flattening each ball, so it looks more like a chicken nugget. Be sure to space them apart, so they do not touch each other.
6. Bake for 20 minutes, remove from the oven, and flip each nugget over with tongs. Return to the oven for 10 more minutes.
7. Cool for a few minutes, and then serve with honey, barbecue sauce, or Ranch dipping sauce.

Nutrition: Calories 245 Fat 4.4g Carbohydrate 41.6g Protein 12.5g

325. Apple Mint Salad with Pine Nut Crunch

Preparation Time: 10 Minutes

Cook Time: 0 Minutes

Servings: 2

Ingredients:

- 1 medium apple, diced
- 1 tablespoon lemon juice
- 1 teaspoon maple syrup
- ½ teaspoon dried mint
- 1 tablespoon fresh pomegranate seeds
- 1 teaspoon pine nuts or sliced almonds

Directions:

1. Toast the nuts in a pan on the stove. Stir constantly so they don't burn and let them turn a golden brown. Set the pan aside until cooled to room temperature.
2. Place the diced apple in a small bowl with the lemon juice and stir around, so all the apple is coated.

3. Add the maple syrup and dried mint and stir it in.

4. Sprinkle the top of the salad with pomegranate seeds and toasted nuts.

Nutrition: Calories 128 Fat 1.3g Carbohydrate 30g Protein 1.1g

326. Pleasant Lemonade

Preparation Time: 10 Minutes

Cooking Time: 3 hours and 15 minutes

Servings: 10

Ingredients:

- Cinnamon sticks for serving
- 2 cups of coconut sugar
- 1/4 cup of honey
- 3 cups of lemon juice. Fresh
- 32 fluid ounce of water

Directions:

1. Using a 4-quarts slow cooker, place all the ingredients except for the cinnamon sticks and stir properly.

2. Cover it with the lid, then plug in the slow cooker and cook it for 3 hours on the low heat setting or until it is heated thoroughly.

3. When done, stir properly and serve with the cinnamon sticks.

Nutrition: Calories: 146 Carbohydrates: 34g Protein: 0g Fats: 0g

327. Soothing Ginger Tea Drink

Preparation Time: 10 Minutes

Cooking Time: 2 hours and 15 minutes

Servings: 8

Ingredients:

- 1 tablespoon of minced gingerroot
- 2 tablespoons of honey
- 15 green tea bags
- 32 fluid ounce of white grape juice
- 2 quarts of boiling water

Directions:

1. Pour water into a 4-quarts slow cooker, immerse tea bags, cover the cooker, and let stand for 10 minutes.

2. After 10 minutes, remove and discard tea bags and stir in the remaining ingredients.

3. Return cover to slow cooker, then plug in and let cook at high heat setting for 2 hours or until heated through.

4. When done, strain the liquid and serve hot or cold.

Nutrition: Calories: 45 Carbohydrates: 12g Protein: 0g Fats: 0g

328. Nice Spiced Cherry Cider

Preparation Time: 10 Minutes

Cooking Time: 4 hours and 5 minutes

Servings: 16

Ingredients:

- 2 cinnamon sticks, each about 3 inches long

- 6-ounce of cherry gelatin
- 4 quarts of apple cider

Directions:

1. Using a 6-quarts slow cooker, pour the apple cider and add the cinnamon stick.

2. Stir, then cover the slow cooker with its lid. Plug in the cooker and let it cook for 3 hours at the high heat setting or until it is heated thoroughly.

3. Then add and stir the gelatin properly, then continue cooking for another hour.

4. When done, remove the cinnamon sticks and serve the drink hot or cold.

Nutrition: Calories: 100 Carbohydrates: 0g Protein: 0g Fats: 0g

329. <u>Fragrant Spiced Coffee</u>

Preparation Time: 10 Minutes

Cooking Time: 2 hours and 10 minutes

Servings: 8

Ingredients:

- 4 cinnamon sticks, each about 3 inches long
- 1 1/2 teaspoons of whole cloves
- 1/3 cup of honey
- 2-ounce of chocolate syrup
- 1/2 teaspoon of anise extract
- 8 cups of brewed coffee

Directions:

1. Pour the coffee into a 4-quarts slow cooker and pour in the remaining

ingredients except for cinnamon and stir properly.

2. Wrap the whole cloves in cheesecloth and tie its corners with strings.

3. Immerse this cheesecloth bag in the liquid present in the slow cooker and cover it with the lid.

4. Then plug in the slow cooker and let it cook on the low heat setting for 3 hours or until heated thoroughly.

5. When done, discard the cheesecloth bag and serve.

Nutrition: Calories: 150 Carbohydrates: 35g Protein: 3g Fats: 0g

330. <u>Tangy Spiced Cranberry Drink</u>

Preparation Time: 10 Minutes

Cooking Time: 2 hours and 10 minutes

Servings: 14

Ingredients:

- 1 1/2 cups of coconut sugar
- 12 whole cloves
- 2 fluid ounce of lemon juice
- 6 fluid ounce of orange juice
- 32 fluid ounce of cranberry juice
- 8 cups of hot water
- 1/2 cup of Red Hot candies

Directions:

1. Pour the water into a 6-quarts slow cooker along with the cranberry juice, orange juice, and lemon juice.

2. Stir the sugar properly.

3. Wrap the whole cloves in a cheesecloth, tie its corners with strings, and immerse it in the liquid present inside the slow cooker.

4. Add the red hot candies to the slow cooker and cover it with the lid.

5. Then plug in the slow cooker and let it cook on the low heat setting for 3 hours or until it is heated thoroughly.

6. When done, discard the cheesecloth bag and serve.

Nutrition: Calories: 89 Carbohydrates: 27g Protein: 0g Fats: 0g

331. **Warm Pomegranate Punch**

Preparation Time: 10 Minutes

Cooking Time: 2 hours and 10 minutes

Servings: 8

Ingredients:

- 3 cinnamon sticks, each about 3 inches long

- 12 whole cloves

- 1/2 cup of coconut sugar

- 1/3 cup of lemon juice

- 32 fluid ounce of pomegranate juice

- 32 fluid ounce of apple juice, unsweetened

- 16 fluid ounce of brewed tea

Directions:

1. Using a 4-quart slow cooker, pour the lemon juice, pomegranate, juice apple juice, tea, and then sugar.

2. Wrap the whole cloves and cinnamon stick in a cheesecloth, tie its corners

with a string, and immerse it in the liquid present in the slow cooker.

3. Then cover it with the lid, plug in the slow cooker and let it cook at the low heat setting for 3 hours or until it is heated thoroughly.

4. When done, discard the cheesecloth bag and serve it hot or cold.

Nutrition: Calories: 253 Carbohydrates: 58g Protein: 7g Fats: 2g

332. **Rich Truffle Hot Chocolate**

Preparation Time: 10 Minutes

Cooking Time: 1 hour and 10 minutes

Servings: 4

Ingredients:

- 1/3 cup of cocoa powder, unsweetened

- 1/3 cup of coconut sugar

- 1/8 teaspoon of salt

- 1/8 teaspoon of ground cinnamon

- 1 teaspoon of vanilla extract, unsweetened

- 32 fluid ounce of coconut milk

Directions:

1. Using a 2 quarts slow cooker, add all the ingredients, and stir properly.

2. Cover it with the lid, then plug in the slow cooker and cook it for 2 hours on the high heat setting or until it is heated thoroughly.

3. When done, serve right away.

Nutrition: Calories: 67 Carbohydrates: 13 Protein: 2g Fats: 2g

333.   Dehydrated Walnuts

Preparation Time: 15 Minutes

Cooking Time: 24 Hours

Servings: 4

Ingredients:

- 1 cup walnuts, soaked overnight and drained
- 2 tablespoons dates, pitted and mashed into a paste form
- 1/8 teaspoon ground cinnamon
- Pinch of cayenne pepper
- Sea salt, as required

Directions:

1. Set the dehydrator to 100 degrees F.
2. In a large bowl, mix together all ingredients.
3. Arrange the walnuts onto the dehydrator sheets.
4. Dehydrate for about 24 hours.
5. Remove from the dehydrator and set aside to cool completely before serving.

Nutrition: Calories: 209 Fats: 18.5g Carbs: 7.4g Proteins: 7.7g

334.   Kale Chips

Preparation Time: 10 Minutes

Cooking Time: 15 minutes

Servings: 6

Ingredients:

- 1 pound fresh kale leaves, stemmed and torn
- ¼ teaspoon cayenne pepper

- Salt, as required
- 1 tablespoon olive oil

Directions:

1. Preheat the oven to 350 degrees F. Line a large baking sheet with a parchment paper.
2. Arrange the kale pieces onto the prepared baking sheet in a single layer.
3. Sprinkle the kale with the cayenne pepper and salt and drizzle with oil.
4. Bake for about 10-15 minutes.
5. Remove from the oven and set aside to cool before serving.

Nutrition: Calories: 57 Fats: 2.3g Carbs: 8g Proteins: 2.3g

335.   Beet Chips

Preparation Time: 15 Minutes

Cooking Time: 30 minutes

Servings: 4

Ingredients:

- 2 medium beets, trimmed, peeled, and sliced thinly
- 1 tablespoon canola oil
- Salt, as required

Directions:

1. Preheat the oven to 350 degrees F. Line 2 large baking sheets with parchment paper.
2. In a large bowl, add the beet slices and oil and toss to coat well.
3. Arrange the beet slices onto the prepared baking sheets in a single layer.

4. Bake for about 20-30 minutes.

5. Remove from the oven and set aside to cool before serving.

Nutrition: Calories: 53 Fats: 3.6g Carbs: 5g Proteins: 0.8g

336. Zucchini Chips

Preparation Time: 15 Minutes

Cooking Time: 15 minutes

Servings: 2

Ingredients:

- 1 medium zucchini, cut into thin slices
- 1/8 teaspoon ground turmeric
- 1/8 teaspoon ground cumin
- Salt, as required
- 2 teaspoons olive oil

Directions:

1. Preheat the oven to 400 degrees F. Line 2 baking sheets with parchment papers.

2. In a large bowl, add all ingredients and toss to coat well.

3. Transfer the mixture onto the prepared baking sheets in a single layer.

4. Bake for about 10-15 minutes.

5. Serve immediately.

Nutrition: Calories: 57 Fats: 4.9g Carbs: 3.4g Proteins: 1.2g

337. Banana Chips

Preparation Time: 15 Minutes

Cooking Time: 1 hour

Servings: 4

Ingredients:

- 2 large bananas, peeled and cut into ¼-inch thick slices
- ½ teaspoon ground cinnamon

Directions:

1. Prepare the oven to 250 degrees F. Line a large baking sheet with a parchment paper.

2. Place the banana slices onto a prepared baking sheet.

3. Bake for about 1 hour.

4. Remove from the oven and set aside to cool before serving.

Nutrition: Calories: 61 Fats: 0.2g Carbs: 15.8g Proteins: 0.8g

338. Dehydrated Oranges

Preparation Time: 10 Minutes

Cooking Time: 10 hours

Servings: 4

Ingredients:

- 2 seedless navel oranges, sliced thinly
- Salt, as required

Directions:

1. Set the dehydrator to 135 degrees F.

2. Arrange the orange slices onto the dehydrator sheets.

3. Dehydrate for about 10 hours.

4. Remove the orange slices from the dehydrator and set aside to cool completely before serving.

Nutrition: Calories: 43 Fats: 0.1g Carbs: 10.8g Proteins: 0.9g

339. Sweet Potato Mash

Preparation Time: 15 Minutes

Cooking Time: 20 minutes

Servings: 4

Ingredients:

- 3 medium sweet potatoes, peeled and cut into 2-inch chunks
- ¼ cup unsweetened almond milk
- 1-2 tablespoons maple syrup
- Salt, as required
- ¼ teaspoon ground cinnamon
- Pinch of ground nutmeg

Directions:

1. In a large pan of boiling water, arrange a steamer basket.
2. Place the sweet potato chunks in the steamer basket.
3. Cover and steam for about 15-20 minutes or until desired doneness.
4. Drain well and transfer the sweet potato chunks into a bowl.
5. With a potato masher, mash the chunks.
6. Add the remaining ingredients and mix until well combined.
7. Serve immediately.

Nutrition: Calories: 142 Fats: 0.4g Carbs: 33.2g Proteins: 1.7g

340. Cauliflower Mash

Preparation Time: 15 Minutes

Cooking Time: 12 minutes

Servings: 3

Ingredients:

- 1 head cauliflower, chopped
- 2 tablespoons homemade vegetable broth
- 2 garlic cloves, chopped
- 2 tablespoons coconut oil
- Salt, as required

Directions:

1. In a microwave-safe bowl, add the cauliflower and broth and microwave on High for about 10-12 minutes.
2. In a food processor, add the cauliflower mixture and remaining ingredients and pulse until smooth.
3. Serve immediately.

Nutrition: Calories: 104 Fats: 9.2g Carbs: 5.5g Proteins: 1.9g

341. Apple Leather

Preparation Time: 15 Minutes

Cooking Time: 12 hours 25 minutes

Servings: 2

Ingredients:

- 1 cup water
- 8 cups apples, peeled, cored and chopped
- 1 tablespoon ground cinnamon
- 2 tablespoons fresh lemon juice

Directions:

1. In a large pan, add water and apples over medium-low heat and simmer for about 10-15 minutes, stirring occasionally.

2. Remove from heat and set aside to cool slightly.

3. In a blender, add apple mixture and pulse until smooth.

4. Return the mixture into the pan over medium-low heat.

5. Stir in cinnamon and lemon juice and simmer for about 10 minutes.

6. Transfer the mixture onto dehydrator trays, and with the back of the spoon smooth the top.

7. Set the dehydrator at 135 degrees F.

8. Dehydrate for about 10-12 hours.

9. Cut the apple leather into equal-sized rectangles.

10. Now, roll each rectangle to make fruit rolls.

Nutrition: Calories: 238 Fats: 0.9g Carbs: 63.1g Proteins: 1.3g

342. Sautéed Brussels Sprout

Preparation Time: 15 minutes

Cooking Time: 15 minutes

Servings: 2

Ingredients:

- ½ pound Brussels sprouts, halved
- 1 tablespoon olive oil
- 2 garlic cloves, minced

- ½ teaspoon red pepper flakes, crushed
- Salt and ground black pepper, as required
- 1 tablespoon fresh lemon juice

Directions:

1. Arrange a steamer basket over a large pan of boiling water.

2. Place the asparagus in a steamer basket. Cover and steam for about 6 to 8 minutes. Drain well.

3. In a large skillet, heat oil over medium heat.

4. Add garlic and red pepper flakes and sauté for about 1 minute.

5. Add the Brussels sprouts, salt, and black pepper, and sauté for 4-5 minutes.

6. Stir in the lemon juice and sauté for 1 minute more.

7. Serve hot.

Nutrition: Calories: 117 Fats: 7.6g Carbs: 11.7g Proteins: 4.2g

343. Green Beans with Mushrooms

Preparation Time: 15 Minutes

Cooking Time: 20 minutes

Servings: 2

Ingredients:

- 2 tablespoons olive oil
- 2 tablespoons yellow onion, minced
- ½ teaspoon garlic, minced

- 1 (8-ounce) package white mushrooms, sliced
- 1 cup frozen green beans
- Salt and ground black pepper, as required

Directions:

1. In a skillet, heat the oil over medium heat and sauté the onion and garlic for about 1 minute.
2. Add the mushrooms and cook for about 6-7 minutes.
3. Stir in the green beans and cook for about 5-10 minutes or until desired doneness.
4. Serve hot.

Nutrition: Calories: 166 Fats: 14.4g Carbs: 8.8g Proteins: 4.7g

344. Pinto Beans with Salsa

Preparation Time: 15 minutes

Cooking Time: 12 minutes

Servings: 4

Ingredients:

- 1 tablespoon canola oil
- 1 small onion, chopped
- 1 garlic clove, minced
- 2 teaspoons fresh cilantro, minced
- 2 (15-ounce) cans pinto beans, rinsed and drained
- 2/3 cup salsa

Directions:

1. In a large skillet, heat the oil over medium heat and sauté the onion for about 4-5 minutes.
2. Add the garlic and cilantro and sauté for about 1 minute.
3. Stir in the beans and salsa and cook for about 4-5 minutes or until heated completely.
4. Serve hot.

Nutrition: Calories: 182 Fats: 4.3g Carbs: 26.4g Proteins: 8.2g

345. Asparagus Soup

Preparation Time: 15 minutes

Cooking Time: 40 minutes

Servings: 4

Ingredients:

- 1 tablespoon olive oil
- 3 scallions, chopped
- 1½ pounds fresh asparagus, trimmed and chopped
- 4 cups homemade vegetable broth
- 2 tablespoons fresh lemon juice
- Salt and ground black pepper, as required

Directions:

1. In a large pan, heat the oil over medium heat and sauté the scallion for about 4-5 minutes.
2. Stir in the asparagus and broth and bring to a boil.
3. Reduce the heat to low and simmer, covered for about 25-30 minutes.

4. Remove from the heat and set aside to cool slightly.

5. Now, transfer the soup into a high-speed blender in 2 batches and pulse until smooth.

6. Return the soup into the same pan over medium heat and simmer for about 4-5 minutes.

7. Stir in the lemon juice, salt, and black pepper and remove from the heat.

8. Serve hot.

Nutrition: Calories: 84 Fats: 3.8g Carbs: 10.6g Proteins: 4g

346. Beet Soup

Preparation Time: 10 minutes

Cooking Time: 5 minutes

Servings: 2

Ingredients:

- 2 cups coconut yogurt

- 4 teaspoons fresh lemon juice

- 2 cups beets, trimmed, peeled and chopped

- 2 tablespoons fresh dill

- Salt, as required

Directions:

1. In a high-speed blender, add all ingredients and pulse until smooth.

2. Transfer the soup into a pan over medium heat and cook for about 3-5 minutes or until heated through.

3. Serve immediately.

Nutrition: Calories: 255 Fats: 11.5g Carbs: 29.9g Proteins: 15.6g

347. Pears in Red Wine Sauce

Preparation Time: 10 minutes

Cooking Time: 10 minutes

Servings: 6

Ingredients:

- 6 pears

- 1 cup of superfine sugar

- 1 wine glass of red wine (5-6 oz.)

- 1 pinch cinnamon

- 1 vanilla pod

- 1 clove bud

Directions:

1. Peel the pears.

2. In a pressure cooker pot, dissolve the sugar in the wine together with vanilla and clove.

3. Place the pears into the pot and close the lid.

4. Cook for 7 minutes on low heat.

Nutrition: Total Carbs 66.7 g Fat 0.5 g Protein 0.8g Calories 277

348. Polenta

Preparation Time: 5 minutes

Cooking Time: 15 minutes

Servings: 6

Ingredients:

- 1 cup polenta (coarse-ground cornmeal)

- 4 cups vegetable broth

- 3–4 tsp. butter

- ½ cup Mexican blend shredded cheese
- ¼ cup half and half
- Salt to taste

Directions:

- Press the "Sauté" function on the Instant Pot. Add the broth and polenta, whisk together.
- When it starts to boil, seal the lid. Select "Manual" and set on high pressure for 7 minutes.
- When the cooking cycle is finished, release the pressure naturally.
- Use a whisk to blend in the butter, cheese, and half and half. It will help to thicken the polenta.
- Salt, if needed, and serve.

Nutrition: Calories 170 Total Carbs 22 g Fat 6 g Protein 5 g

349. Carrots in Thyme

Preparation Time: 10 minutes

Cooking Time: 5 minutes

Servings: 4

Ingredients

- 4 carrots, peeled
- 1½ tsp. fresh thyme
- 2 Tbsp. butter
- ½ cup water
- 1 dash salt

Directions:

- Melt butter in the pressure cooker over medium heat.

- Cut the peeled carrots into sticks (like French fries).
- Add the carrots, thyme, salt, and ½ cup of water to the pot.
- Cover and cook at high pressure for 1 minutes, then turn off the heat and let sit for 4 min.
- Release the pressure gently. Serve.

Nutrition: Total Carbs 6 g Fat 5.8 g Protein 0.6 g Calories 77

350. Smoky Pecan Brussels sprouts

Preparation Time: 5 minutes

Cooking Time: 10 minutes

Servings: 2

Ingredients:

- 2 cups small baby Brussels sprouts
- ¼ cup water
- ½ tsp. liquid smoke
- ¼ cup pecans, chopped
- 2 Tbsps. maple syrup
- Salt and pepper to taste

Directions:

- Add water, Brussels sprouts, and liquid smoke to an Instant Pot, mix well.
- Lock the lid and close the pressure valve. Cook on high pressure for 2 minutes.
- When the cooking time is up, release the pressure manually.

- Select the "Sauté" function and add the pecans and maple syrup. Reduce the liquid as you finish cooking the sprouts. Once the sprouts are tender, remove from the heat.

- Salt and pepper to taste and serve.

Nutrition: Calories 113 Total Carbs 17 g Fat 3 g Protein 5 g

CONCLUSION

Well done! Thank you for reaching the end of this book, The Complete Vegetarian Cookbook.

Hopefully, this book has helped you understand that making vegetarian recipes and diet easier can improve your life, not only by improving your health and helping you lose weight, but also by saving you money and time.

Remember that vegetarianism is a choice, not a religion.

Be flexible when it comes to your diet and enjoy new tastes and experiences.

Don't be afraid of meat substitutes, but experiment with using them sparingly. There is no need to completely replace meat with fake meat products like tofu or processed soy-based vegetarian burgers and hot dogs. Not only are they expensive, but fake meats contain artificial ingredients that may or may not be healthy for you.

Also, if you are not used to eating a vegetarian diet, start with a few vegetarian meals and snacks during the week, and see how you feel.

You can always add more vegetarian meals to your diet later. It is better to be even slightly vegetarians than completely non-vegetarian.

The best tip I can give you about making vegetarian recipes is to experiment and have fun!

Here are some more tips to help you with your vegetarian diet:

1. Remember that vegetarianism is not a destination, it is a journey.

2. A vegetarian diet is plant-based. This means that you should try to eat more plants and less animal products. You should also be careful not to replace whole foods with their processed counterparts, such as replacing whole foods such as fruits and vegetables with fruit juice and pasta sauce.

3. Try to avoid processed food whenever possible, while still maintaining your balanced diet and nutrients that you need for your health. An easier way of doing this will be to make your own food when possible and try to avoid packaged, pre-prepared foods at the grocery store.

4. Avoid processed food products that contain artificial ingredients, such as sweeteners, colors, and flavors.

5. Avoid highly processed meat substitutes. Remember to use meat substitutes in moderation or as an occasional treat.

6. If you choose to eat meat substitutes such as tofu, be sure to thoroughly cook it and try different ways of preparing it

7. You may need to gradually introduce your family and friends to your new eating habits. Don't expect everyone to support you or enjoy the same things you do when it comes to vegetarian recipes. As long as you are happy with your food choices, that is the most important thing – even if it means making some changes at home!

When you are having a hard time, always remember this: You can always choose to stop being a vegetarian.

You can simply start eating meat again if you are struggling with your new diet.

Remember that it is okay to be a part-time vegetarian, but if you find that you cannot maintain the lifestyle or are unhappy with your choice, it is always better to go back to eating a non-veg diet.

There is no shame in making changes to your vegetarian recipe routine if you need to, and you will not shame yourself for deciding that a strict vegetarian diet does not work for you.

I know that there are many books and choosing my book is amazing. I am thankful that you stopped and took the time to decide. You made a great decision, and I am sure that you enjoyed it.

I will be even happier if you will add some comments. Feedbacks helped by growing, and they still do. They help me to choose better content and new ideas. So, maybe your feedback can trigger an idea for my next book. Thank you again for downloading this book!

I hope you enjoyed reading my book!

Printed in Great Britain
by Amazon